PRAISE FOR LIFE K

"It didn't take me long to get hooked reading this must-have guide-book for parents who want to help their children combat peer pressure and bullying. Unlike other temporary, band-aid solutions, this book will truly help your child develop the kind of inner confidence and resilience that cannot be bullied away. Children will love the simple, empowering strategies."

—**Jane Nelsen, EdD, author of** *Positive Discipline*

"This book is for any parent concerned about building their child's self-esteem (what parent isn't?), but not with trophies, stickers, and 'good job' accolades. The Hewitts understand where true self-esteem comes from and offer clear, easy, and kid-friendly steps for guiding even the shyest child toward self-confidence and assertiveness, first by accepting and acknowledging whatever life puts in front of them. This is where education should start. If it did, we would be raising communities of kind, responsible, caring citizens."

—**Bonnie Harris, director of Connective Parenting and author of** *Confident Parents, Remarkable Kids* **and** *When Your Kids Push Your Buttons*

"This book is a breath of fresh air. Jonathan and Lana Hewitt give parents practical, easy-to-implement strategies to give kids what they need most—happiness from the inside out. Highly recommended for any parent who wants to foster *internal* motivation and prepare their kids to handle the challenges of life with resilience, confidence, and courage."

—**Amy McCready, author of** *If I Have to Tell You One More Time…*

Life Ki-do
PARENTING

TOOLS *to* RAISE HAPPY, CONFIDENT
KIDS *from the* INSIDE OUT

JONATHAN & LANA HEWITT

RIVER GROVE
BOOKS

The information given here is not intended as a substitute for any professional medical advice. It is provided for educational purposes only.

Published by River Grove Books
Austin, TX
www.greenleafbookgroup.com

Distributed by River Grove Books

For ordering information or special discounts for bulk purchases, please contact River Grove Books at PO Box 91869, Austin, TX 78709, 512.891.6100.

Author photos by Photographers of West Lake
Illustrations by Marci Boone
Design and composition by Greenleaf Book Group LLC
Cover design by Greenleaf Book Group LLC
Cover photo ©Jupterimages/Brand X Pictures/Getty Images

Publisher's Cataloging-In-Publication Data
(Prepared by The Donohue Group, Inc.)
Hewitt, Jonathan (Jonathan Andrew)
    Life ki-do parenting : tools to raise happy, confident kids from the inside out / Jonathan & Lana Hewitt. -- 1st ed.
        p. ; cm.
    Issued also as an ebook.
    Includes bibliographical references.
    ISBN: 978-1-938416-06-4
    1. Child rearing. 2. Happiness in children. 3. Confidence in children. 4. Success in children. 5. Martial arts for children. I. Hewitt, Lana. II. Title. III. Title: Parenting
HQ769 .H485 2012
649/.1

LCCN: 2012909871
Print ISBN: 978-1-938416-06-4
eBook ISBN: 978-1-938416-08-8
First Edition

LOVINGLY DEDICATED

To our precious daughter, Emilia Wendy,

who brings more love, laughter, and joy to our lives than we ever could have imagined

IN GRATITUDE

To our parents Barry and Wendy, Nick and Emily for giving us roots and wings

To our amazing Life Ki-do team for helping to make all of this work possible

To the wonder and miracle of life itself

CONTENTS

CHAPTER 1

THE FOUNDATIONS OF THE SYSTEM

To be healthy and happy. That's the answer most parents give when asked what they want for their children. It sounds simple enough. Yet today our children seem to be getting farther and farther away from those two ideals. Studies have shown that today's generation of children might be the first ever to live a shorter life than their parents' generation, indicating critical health issues.[1] On the happiness scale, we are doing no better. Remarkably, children were significantly less anxious and depressed during the Great Depression and World War II than they are today.[2] Clearly, something is wrong. Something is missing. Change needs to happen: We must find a way to steer our children back on the path to health and happiness.

While the solution to the health issue is certainly not a simple one, there are basic guidelines for diet and exercise that can have profound positive effects on our children. It's a matter of parents and children following those guidelines. When it comes to the happiness component, however, the answers don't seem to be quite so obvious. Where are the guidelines for us to follow? What are the basics—the "diet and exercise" formula—to raising happy children?

I have been searching my entire life for the answers to this question. After twenty-five years of personal introspection, earning a degree in psychology, endless study of ancient wisdom and martial arts principles, as well as years of practical application in teaching thousands of children, I have distilled everything I've learned into a concise life system for children. A life system that gives parents the tools and critical skills necessary to raise a confident, resilient, and caring child. This system—the Life Ki-do® Tools for Life— is the "diet and exercise" formula for living a happy life.

MY STORY

My own story not only greatly influenced the creation of the Life Ki-do system, but I think it's quite indicative of the way many of us look for happiness. I was star of the soccer field as a child, state wrestling champion as a teenager, and a commercial model and promising Wall Street intern as a young adult. Yet not one of these achievements gave me the confidence and fulfillment I was looking for. In fact, as early as the age of seven I started getting daily stress-related stomachaches and migraine headaches.

I was following what I now call the American Happiness Formula. Back then I didn't have a label for it, and it wasn't spelled out for me. Yet the formula ruled my life and the lives of those around me. It was unspoken, yet it was accepted by most, if not all. Today I can clearly decipher the formula: Look Good + Perform Well + Get Approval = Happiness.

I tried my best to perfect this formula. It was without a doubt my path in life, and to outsiders it looked like I had it all. But somehow this method never added up to the happiness I expected. My efforts to achieve happiness left me feeling empty and frustrated; I was working backward, from the outside in.

My brother also worked hard to make this formula work for him. Like me he didn't find the happiness that he hoped for. Yet when the American Happiness Formula didn't produce his desired results, he assumed that it was because of his inability to perform the formula correctly instead of realizing that it was the formula itself that was the problem. He felt that he lacked the ability to look good enough, perform well enough, and get the right approval. He was so hard on himself for not living up to the formula that he became utterly despondent and lost all hope. The pressure became unbearable for him and he wanted out. So much so, that one day I came home to find him alone in the house after attempting to take his own life.

I didn't know at first what was happening. My brother seemed groggy and insisted that he just wanted to sleep and be left alone. But somehow I knew something wasn't right. I persisted in questioning him, and he finally admitted that he had taken a lot of pills. I was terrified and knew that I needed to race him to the hospital. To my great relief, I managed to get him there in time to save his life. But life itself was never the same for him or for me. Something *had* to change. We both needed answers.

After that harrowing incident, I changed the direction of the path I was on. I decided not to pursue a Wall Street career and I switched my degree from economics to psychology, from the study of currency to the study of humanity. Please don't get me wrong. There's nothing wrong with looking good, making money, and having a successful career. But I realized that my approach in fixating on these outer circumstances would not lead me to the inner happiness and fulfillment I craved. I realized that my true fulfillment needed to come from the inside out, and finding how to achieve that became my life's purpose.

I read, I studied, and I spent hours in deep meditation. I practiced martial arts, and I became a sensei—a martial arts instructor. Years went by and slowly and consistently a profound inner transformation took place. That inner peace and fulfillment continues to expand and deepen to this day. Everything I was looking for by trying to look good, be the best, and get approval I found within myself.

Naturally my journey and the answers I was finding started spilling over into my role as a martial arts instructor for children. The teaching became about so much more than just kicking and punching. Through the years, it was these life skills that attracted thousands of children to come through the doors of my academy. Children loved my classes because they felt so good about themselves, and parents loved that they could see real and deep positive transformation in their children.

Parents started asking me how they could reinforce at home what their children were learning in my classes. They told me about the parenting books they were reading and that those books all focused on what they as parents should and shouldn't do in response to certain behavior from their children. They told me that there was plenty out there about how to handle behavior or, should I say, misbehavior. But something was missing. They wanted to know how to empower their children like I was able to do in my martial arts classes. Parents wanted to give their children the skills to be happy, confident, and resilient.

I realized that the time had come for me to organize my teachings into a life system that would give children the answers I had been so desperately looking for in my own childhood. This was a full circle for me, and I felt that a life system would give parents the missing link they were looking for. So I drew upon the ancient wisdom of martial arts and wise men, added in the knowledge I had garnered from years of studying modern psychology and human development, and filtered all of this material through what I had actually seen succeed in my twenty years of teaching thousands of children of all ages.

I knew from my years of teaching martial arts that the best way for a student to learn a physical skill was for me to break it down into a few easy steps that they could understand, remember, and make their own. I used that same philosophy to break down the life skill material. What I found was that for children to be happy and fulfilled they must develop from the inside out four essential life skills: Focus and Mindfulness, Confidence and a Strong Sense of Self, Resilience and the Ability to Deal with Life's Challenges, and Social Intelligence. Out with the American Happiness Formula and in with the Life Ki-do Happiness Formula.

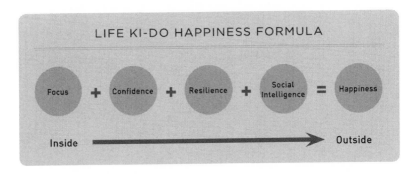

I knew that identifying the four skills for happiness wasn't enough. I knew that I needed to give parents and children a tangible, kid-friendly way to practice and implement these skills. So I created the Life Ki-do Tools for Life system, four simple life tools to help children develop each of the four essential life skills.

One of my six-year-old students once said to me, "You are teaching kids how to live a better life." That's it! He got it. And I got it too. All of those years of angst I experienced as a child, the inner turmoil I saw my brother consumed by, the studying, the training, the teaching—it was all worth it. My search had become my path, my purpose, and my passion.

WHY IT WORKS

Of course you want your child to be happy. Research shows that happy children are more independent, more enthusiastic, better at problem solving, and have more friends. Yet we are faced with a big problem today. Rates of anxiety, depression, and suicide among children and adolescents have been increasing steadily for the past fifty to seventy years. According to the Centers for Disease Control and Prevention, suicide is the third leading cause of death for youth between the ages of ten and twenty-four.

Jean Twenge, professor at San Diego State University, has conducted extensive research on mental illness and mental distress across generations. She says that the rate of depression is a whopping ten times higher today than in 1915, and the suicide rate for children under the age of fourteen has doubled since just 1980. Remarkably, her research shows that the time period a child is born in actually has greater impact on his level of anxiety than even his family environment. For example, college students in the 1990s were more anxious than 85 percent of students in the 1950s. Shockingly, average schoolchildren in the 1980s reported higher levels of anxiety than child psychiatric patients in the 1950s. Twenge concludes, "So even if you come from a stable, loving family, growing up amidst the stress of recent times might be enough to make you anxious."[3] With the stress of modern-day living at an all-time high, the alarming rates of youth anxiety, depression, and suicide are sad and disheartening. Something must be done. It's time for change.

As you know, I spent my childhood following the widely accepted but not articulated American Happiness Formula. It failed me, it failed my brother, and I know it has failed countless others. But why? Why doesn't looking good, performing well, and getting approval equal happiness?

It's because these three goals are extrinsically based, requiring one to look to others for happiness and fulfillment. Did others think I looked good? Did I get approval for this, that, or the other thing? Those of us who followed this formula became approval junkies always looking for the next fix, the next hit of validation and approval.

I wasn't the only one. A research study published by Jean Twenge showed that the average young person in 2002 was more externally motivated than 80 percent of young people in the 1960s.[4] When comparing the data, she saw that the rise in children having extrinsic goals matched the same rise in depression and anxiety during the same forty-two-year period. It makes perfect sense to me. These scientific results undoubtedly match my own personal experience.

Because extrinsic goals are based on what other people think of us, we have much less control over achieving these types of goals than intrinsic goals, which are based on a person's individual development. So when children believe they have little or no control over their fate, they become anxious, and when their anxiety and sense of helplessness becomes overwhelming, they become depressed. Children can quickly lose all hope just as my brother did.

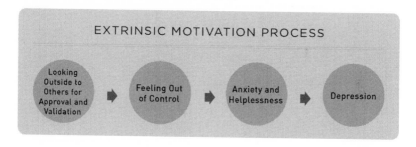

So now that we understand why the American Happiness Formula isn't a happy one at all, let's take a look at what *can* make us happy and fulfilled. If we focus on intrinsic goals, we are looking to personal effort and progress—things we can control. Having a sense of control of our own lives can then lead to feelings of contentment and happiness.

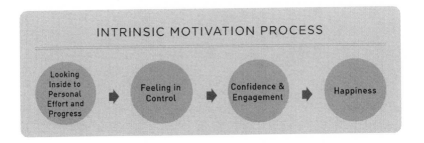

Researchers have shown that those who are intrinsically motivated exhibit not only more interest, excitement, and confidence in their lives but also enhanced performance and higher levels of self-esteem and well-being.[5] There's no doubt that once I made the switch to focusing on internal motivation and fulfillment rather than constantly looking to others, my whole life changed.

In my younger years as a martial artist and state wrestling champion, my focus was on everything external. It was all about using my physical strength and physical moves to beat my opponent, who I saw not as a fellow human being but rather as a roadblock to being the best. I saw myself only in comparison to others. Were my kicks higher? Were my punches faster? Could I take down someone bigger than me?

However, as my personal journey evolved, so did my training in martial arts. While many people associate the martial arts only with fighting, aggression, and competition, traditional martial arts actually teach respect, discipline, focus, honor, and courage. Steeped in ancient traditions and an emphasis on the integration of mind and body, martial arts is truly an art. It's the art of finding oneself—finding one's inner strength and inner peace.

For me personally, it was the Russian art of Systema that took my experience of martial arts to a much deeper level. While you are training your body, Systema asks you to turn inward and focus on breath, relaxation, and sensitivity. Systema teaches one how to be free of tension, anger, fear, pride, and self-pity and how to enter a state of humility, calmness, and caring for others. Through the breath and fluid movements of the body, you are taught to work through your limitations in order to develop an inner strength that becomes one's foundation for living.

My first day of training with Russian master Vladimir Vasiliev certainly gave me a glimpse into the deeper work of Systema. The first four and a half hours were nothing but push-ups, sit-ups, squats, and leg raises. I was astounded at what my body was capable of. Vladimir wasn't teaching us how to do the perfect push-up; he was helping us to dig deep within ourselves to discover how our breath and inner strength could affect our physical might, endurance, and resilience. I found that I was no longer comparing myself to others. It wasn't about anyone else. It wasn't about being the best. It was about finding my own inner strength—a strength that no one could touch and a strength that would spill over into every aspect of my life.

Naturally, I knew that I needed to find a way to empower children to find their own inner strength, even if they had no prior training in martial arts. So I created the Life Ki-do Tools for Life to help children look inward to monitor themselves rather than looking outward to others for their validation and self-worth.

I knew there was one more important ingredient necessary to make a happy child. We are not alone in this world, and thus a strong sense of self needs to be coupled with a caring heart so that children can interact with others in a positive and healthy manner.

Psychologist Edward Diener is considered by many to be the world's foremost expert on the science of happiness and life satisfaction and has thus earned the moniker "Dr. Happiness." A study by Diener and Martin Seligman, founder of Positive Psychology, showed that the students they surveyed who displayed the highest levels of happiness and fewest signs of depression had strong, good-quality relationships with friends and family and maintained a commitment to cultivating those relationships.[6] Diener claims that "it is important to work on social skills, close interpersonal ties, and social support in order to be happy."[7] Because social relationships have an overwhelming influence on a child's happiness and fulfillment, I made sure that one of the life tools focuses on social intelligence—how to interact with people through mutual acknowledgment, care, and respect.

HOW IT WORKS

We teach our children how to read and write, how to do math, and the basics of history and the sciences. But when do we teach children how to live? What our children really need to learn is a simple step-by-step system that can help them live a happier, more fulfilled life. That's what Life Ki-do Parenting is all about.

What does *Life Ki-do* mean? Well, *ki* (KEE) can be translated to "inner strength or spirit," and *do* (DOH) means "the way." I use the word *life* in this context to mean "your relationship with yourself, others, and the world around you." So *Life Ki-do* means "the way of living from your own inner strength and spirit and honoring the same in others."

The Life Ki-do system for children is simple yet comprehensive. The system is broken down into four tools—River Check-in, River Effort, A–B Formula, and My Shoes, Your Shoes, Our Shoes.

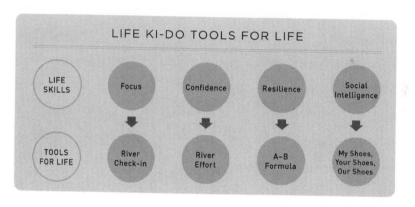

These Tools for Life can be used by children not only in their daily living but also into adulthood and for an entire life span. If you are wondering if that means that these tools can benefit you as the parent as well, you are absolutely correct. While the tools are written in kid-friendly language, the concepts behind them are ancient and universal. They are principles practiced by monks, warriors, and wise men throughout time. These principles and practices transformed my life and continue to be the foundation from which I live today. Even young children can see the value these tools will bring to them as adults. One day I was teaching the Tools for Life to two young girls, ages eight and twelve. Afterward, the eight-year-old suggested, "If people learned this when they were young, they would have much less problems when they were grown-ups." The twelve-year-old added, "That's because what you learn when you are young is how you are when you are older." The wisdom and insight of children never ceases to amaze me!

Designed as a guidebook that is practical and easy for you to implement, *Life Ki-do Parenting* has one chapter devoted to each of the four Tools for Life. I'll explain why the tool works and how specifically the tool can benefit your child. Each tool is broken down into a few concise steps using kid-friendly language proven to appeal to children, making it not only easy for them to understand and remember but, more important, easy for them to apply. You'll find this system simple, basic, and easy to learn but profound in its impact on your child and her path to a happy and successful life.

Teaching your child the four Tools for Life is like teaching him to tie his shoelaces. You teach your child the steps to do it, and after some practice he doesn't even have to think about it. Tying shoelaces becomes second nature. You have empowered your child with a skill he needs to dress himself, and he feels good about himself for having learned how to do it. This is how Tools for Life works. A second grader from an elementary school that adopted Tools for Life happily told the vice-principal, "I use these tools so much that I forget I'm using them!" This happens in the same way he has forgotten that he is using the skills he learned to tie his shoes. It just happens. It becomes part of him.

One day one of my eight-year-old students was having extreme abdominal pain. When his parents took him to the emergency room, the doctors determined he needed an emergency appendectomy. His mother told us afterward that she was amazed that her son immediately defaulted to the breathing techniques he had learned from his Life Ki-do training. No one had to remind him; no one had to calm him down. This tool had become part of his personal internal toolbox and was a natural response to a scary and painful situation. His parents were so grateful that their son had been empowered with the tools to deal with life, because that day life had thrown them a curveball.

Another parent once said about my program, "This is the best gift I have ever given to my kids." It is my sincerest hope that this book will be the same for your child, giving her the foundation to life that I was missing, that my brother was missing, and that so many others have been searching for. I truly believe that with this system you will spend less time micromanaging, your child will feel more respected, empowered, and good about who she is, and your family will become happier and more peaceful.

CHAPTER 2

THE SYSTEM AND HOW
TO PARENT WITH IT

You don't really understand human nature unless you know

why a child on a merry-go-round will wave at his parents every

time around—and why his parents will always wave back.

—William D. Tammeus

So what's the action plan? As we now know, research and studies illustrate that intrinsic motivation leads to empowerment and a strong sense of self—key components to developing happiness and fulfillment. But we need more than just the why. We need the how.

Children (and adults for that matter!) need a blueprint to follow. So I have designed a simple action plan. Life Ki-do Tools for Life is a complete system that empowers children with four easy-to-learn tools. To make it even easier for children to follow and remember, I have broken down each tool into a few, simple steps.

The system terminology not only needed to be descriptive and playful for kids but also to include words that children could relate to and use to easily identify and process their feelings. For example, the word *River* is a main theme in all the tools. I use River because kids can visualize it and understand its implied qualities of being strong yet fluid, always flowing and moving around obstacles, and always moving toward something greater. One day I asked a group of kindergarten children who they thought would win a wrestling match—a rock or a river. They all screamed out river. When I asked why they had chosen river, they told me that the river could move around the rock and could eventually wear it down. To be strong yet fluid at the same time is a beautiful way to live, giving one both the confidence and the flexibility to deal with life.

We will devote one chapter to each of the four Tools for Life, but first I wanted to give you a quick overview of the tools as a total system. The First Tool, River Check-in, helps children to be focused, present, and mindful. Being focused and mindful is an invaluable skill to learn and is a great starting point for accomplishing all things. With a focused mind-set intact, the Second Tool, River Effort, helps children to put forth their best effort when engaging in an activity. This develops self-confidence because the child has a means to internally monitor his own quantity and quality of effort, rather than looking solely to external conditions to validate his experience. But as we all know, even if we are focused and doing our best, life always manages to present challenges, and children need to know how to successfully navigate through them. So the Third Tool, A–B Formula, helps children develop resilience and the ability to work through challenges. Finally, the Fourth Tool, My Shoes, Your Shoes, Our Shoes, helps children develop social intelligence. In addition to having a strong sense of self, having positive and healthy relationships is a critical component to living a happy and fulfilled life.

The following graphic outlines the Tools for Life and the life skills they develop. In quotes is the verbiage I use when explaining the benefits to children.

TOOL #1: RIVER CHECK-IN—3 Bs

Develops Focus by Practicing Mindfulness of the Body, Breath, and Brain

"Helps you to focus on what you are doing"

TOOL #2: RIVER EFFORT—ICE, PUDDLE, RIVER

Develops Confidence and a Strong Sense of Self

"Helps you to feel and be your best"

TOOL #3: A-B FORMULA

Develops Resilience and the Ability to Deal with Life's Challenges

"Helps you when you are having a hard time with what you are feeling or doing"

TOOL #4: MY SHOES, YOUR SHOES, OUR SHOES

Develops Social Intelligence

"Helps you to be a good friend to yourself and to others, and to work as a team"

PRACTICAL TIPS

A general tip for the parent is to remember that the reason these tools work and that children like to use them is that the tools make children feel empowered. As you probably know, children have a sixth sense, and they will know if you are introducing these tools in order to manipulate or control them in any way. Thus, it's critical that your intention or motive when introducing and using these tools is to actually help your child develop her inner strength and not to manipulate her into behaving in a specific way.

Second, as a general rule it's more difficult for your child to first learn these tools if he is in a heightened emotional state. Many studies have shown that humans are more likely to learn and retain information when they are in a more relaxed mental and emotional state. So, for example, it's best not to introduce these tools during a power struggle with your child. If you do, your child may become defensive and reactive, because in that moment he is operating in the emotional part of the brain rather than the rational part of the brain. The tool may then carry a negative connotation for the child. To be clear, the tools are very helpful during heightened emotional states, but I am talking here specifically about the first time you introduce them.

Finally, my suggestion is to focus on one tool at a time. After you've understood and practiced a tool yourself, then introduce it to your child and practice it together for a week, a month, or however long it takes until you and your child feel comfortable with it. Then move to the next tool. This process will help your child integrate the tool and will give her time to see how it can be applied to and benefit many areas of her life.

Do the tools need to be introduced to your child in the order they are presented in this book? There is a logical sequence to the four tools that starts with being focused, moves to putting your heart into all of your actions, then deals with challenges that might arise, and finishes with having healthy social interactions with others. However, each tool stands alone and if need be, you can introduce the tools in the order that seems best for you and your family.

YOUR APPROACH TO PARENTING

To be the most successful in teaching these tools to your children, I believe it is important that your approach to parenting support the philosophy behind the tools. Namely that the child feels empowered and intrinsically motivated to take responsibility in his life.

Behavior modification, using rewards and punishments, seems to be quite a popular parenting approach. But bribing your child with rewards or punishments is really doing your child quite a disservice. It is disempowering because it teaches children that someone else is responsible for their motivation and how they should behave and feel about themselves. Used over and over, these methods train children to become dependent solely on the feedback they are getting from the external world. What they show to the world to get the reward or avoid the punishment might not be what they are feeling on the inside. This internal split can set up relationships with parents and others that feel dishonest, disconnected, and therefore unfulfilling. And as we know by now, anyone who is motivated primarily by external sources can be sucked into the cycle that ends in anxiety and depression.

University of Rochester psychologists Richard Ryan and Edward Deci believe that children are born with a need to have input and control over their own lives, and moreover, that they have a natural inner gauge to do so. When we as parents fill children's lives with rewards and punishments, we are slowly suppressing their need for autonomy and their ability to follow their inner gauge.[1]

But how can giving your child a reward be all bad? In another study Deci showed that a person's intrinsic motivation is weakened not only by punishment but also by rewards, especially if the rewards are perceived as controlling.[2] This is because if someone is given a reward for a task, the tendency is for her to believe that her good performance was a response to the promise of an external reward rather than due to her own internal interest or ability.

Also it has been shown that when children perform for external rewards, their interest in the actual activity declines. In a study of young children published by the *Journal of Personality and Social Psychology*, Mark R. Lepper, David Greene, and Richard E. Nisbett, professors from Stanford University and the University of Michigan, clearly illustrate this point. The children were randomly assigned to three different groups and asked to participate in a drawing task. The first group was rewarded for their task and was told in advance that they would receive a reward. The second group was also rewarded for their task but had no knowledge of the reward until after the task was completed. The third group neither expected nor received an award. Once the study ended and the children no longer received rewards for drawing, which group do you think had the least interest in continuing the task? That's right—the first group. Those children who had expected a reward the first time around showed a decreased interest in the activity once the reward was no longer offered. That's because the first time they were motivated to do the activity was to obtain an extrinsic reward rather than for their own pleasure and personal satisfaction. Those children who had not expected a reward showed either the same or increased interest.[3] With the reward system, children are ultimately learning that the point of being good is to get a reward, rather than learning that doing their best will give them the most fulfillment.

Punishment is just the flip side of the coin. Punishment teaches children to focus on the consequence or penalty they will experience rather than doing their best or on how their actions may be hurting themselves or others. The behavior may stop initially but will most often continue later on. Why? Because the reason the child stopped the misbehavior was extrinsic—someone outside of the child was monitoring and judging the behavior and doling out the punishment. If the reason the child stopped the behavior had been an intrinsic one in which he truly saw and understood the natural consequences of his own behavior, then the child would be much more likely to discontinue that behavior in the future.

One of my fourth-grade students who had a considerable amount of Life Ki-do training mentioned to me that he was no longer bullying children at school. I said, "That's great. Were you bullying kids before?" He said, "Yes," so I asked what made him decide to stop. He told me that he realized how sad and upset he was making others feel, and he also realized that he wasn't feeling his best when he was teasing or provoking others. So he decided to stop the bullying behavior. This kind of intrinsic motivation is invaluable and inherently longer lasting than a quick punishment from a parent or teacher.

So what is the alternative to using rewards and punishments, and how do we deal with our parental addiction to this type of discipline? I believe that there are four pillars to developing a positive approach to parenting: Modeling, Unconditional Love and Acceptance, Nurturing and Empowering Encouragement, and Empowering Discipline. Before you learn the Tools for Life, it's a good idea to get a basic understanding of the Life Ki-do Parenting Pillars.

PARENTING PILLAR #1: MODELING

Have you ever seen the look on a parent's face when his or her toddler says a "bad" word? That look is as much guilt as it is embarrassment: everyone knows that the toddler is most likely copying a word that he heard from one of his parents. We all know that from the time they are infants, our children learn by watching us and mimicking our behavior. Now science knows why. Brain research in the 1990s discovered a new class of pre-motor neurons dubbed mirror neurons. When we watch someone do something, our mirror neurons fire at an incredible rate, helping us to understand and mimic the actions of others. Some have affectionately called these the "monkey see, monkey do" nerve cells.

I'm sure you can see where I'm going with this. If you want your child to learn the Life Ki-do Tools for Life, it's best if you first learn and practice them yourself. Your example is going to be a potent teaching method. As mentioned before, while these tools were written for children using kid-friendly language, they are equally effective and powerful for adults. "Wow! I need to use these skills in my own life!" is a statement I have heard countless times from parents watching their child's class at my academy.

This happens outside the academy as well. A mom told me that one day she was driving and experiencing some mama road rage. Her four-year-old, one of my students, piped up from the backseat and calmly suggested that she just needed to do her *Ninja Breathing*. The mom was humbled, grateful, and a little embarrassed! Many parents have told me similar stories about how their children instruct them on the tools and display an attitude of incredulousness that their parent hadn't thought of it first.

My tips for the most effective modeling are to *Be Genuine* and to *Get Personal*. To *Be Genuine* means that what you say and what you do is congruent with what you are feeling. Your child will know if you are faking it, and pretending will send a confusing message. When I say *Get Personal*, I am suggesting you share your successes and challenges with your children. But of course, it's paramount to be age appropriate and to always keep in mind your role as parent. Never burden your child with more than he or she can handle.

I can't emphasize enough how important it is for your children to see how you deal with your emotions, your challenges, and your interpersonal relationships. This doesn't mean you have to be perfect. In fact, children need to know that everyone makes mistakes and that everyone has feelings of sadness, frustration, anger, etc. It's how you deal with your challenges that's important.

You might say something like, "I had a very frustrating day at work. Now that I think about it, I really don't think I was doing my River Effort. I think I was being much too Icy, but tomorrow I will try to put my heart into what I'm doing to see if I can be more like a River."

I remember telling my students about a seminar I had been to where I was tired and having a hard time focusing. I explained how I did a River Check-in to feel more awake and present and to really absorb the material. I didn't have to tell them explicitly that they should do the same in their school classroom. Their little mirror neurons did that job for me.

While it's great to share stories like this with your children, it's equally important that they see how you act and react while they are with you. Again, this doesn't mean you have to be perfect. Almost any situation can be a teaching moment—using My Shoes, Your Shoes, Our Shoes to understand why the cashier at the grocery store might be exceptionally slow; using the A–B Formula when you are lost and need to find directions; using River Effort to help when you are being a Puddle and procrastinating. Remember that not everything has to be a grand explanation; it's the little moments that often count the most.

I feel confident that if you model these tools in your own life, your family not only will have a common vocabulary of life skills but also will feel more unified, peaceful, and fulfilled.

PARENTING PILLAR #1— MODELING

1. BE GENUINE
   a. Your words are congruent with your feelings
   b. Your actions are congruent with your words
2. GET PERSONAL
   a. Share your successes and challenges
   b. Be age appropriate

PARENTING PILLAR #2: UNCONDITIONAL LOVE AND ACCEPTANCE

In his book, *Self-Esteem: The Costs and Causes of Low Self-Worth*, professor Nicholas Emler concludes from his studies that besides genetic predisposition, a person's self-esteem as a child and into adulthood is most impacted by her parents and whether her parents love, respect, and accept her. Yikes! That's a double whammy. Since you have no control over the DNA that you've handed over to your child, don't stress about the genes your child inherited from you or play the familiar "she must have gotten that from your side of the family" game with your spouse. But given the enormous impact you have, you can commit to giving your child the Unconditional Love and Acceptance she needs to develop a strong, positive self-esteem that will last a lifetime.

A relationship with your child that is founded on Unconditional Love and Acceptance means your child knows and feels at his core that he is loved for who he is and not for what he did or didn't do. Don't misunderstand me. This doesn't mean that you become a pushover and approve of all behavior, or that you can't get upset or angry with your child. It does mean, however, that you don't withdraw or give love as a result of your child's behavior.

Psychologist Carl Rogers (1902–1987), regarded as one of the founding fathers of psychotherapy research, first advocated what he called unconditional positive regard more than fifty years ago. He strongly believed that parents should love their children unconditionally. He believed if a child is not given unconditional love and acceptance, then she will become uncomfortable expressing her feelings and will be afraid to make mistakes for fear of being rejected by her parents. The child learns to abandon her genuine feelings or desires in exchange for seeking approval from her parents. This often leads to an inability to trust and to truly know herself.

If your child doesn't feel your Unconditional Love and Acceptance, he will be prone to becoming overly dependent on you. Since he doesn't feel total acceptance, the child will turn to you at every corner for your feedback on how he should feel.

However, if you give your child Unconditional Love and Acceptance, she can more readily love and accept herself, thus developing her confidence and self-worth. She will feel secure knowing that your love is not going to be withheld and will thus be less afraid to take risks or make mistakes. She will feel more comfortable expressing her true feelings and in turn develop a strong self-identity. Your parent-child relationship will be based on openness, trust, and mutual respect.

Tangible steps you can take are to *Give Unconditional Love* and *Accept Each Child for Who He Is*. To *Give Unconditional Love* means to listen and speak to your child with love and respect and not withdraw your love as a punishment or hand it out as a reward. To *Accept Each Child for Who He Is*, understand that each child is unique, and then imagine how things look from your child's point of view. And remember that *accept* doesn't mean "agree." You can disapprove of your child's behavior without rejecting the whole child.

PARENTING PILLAR #2—
UNCONDITIONAL LOVE & ACCEPTANCE

1. GIVE UNCONDITIONAL LOVE
   a. Listen and speak to your child with love and respect
   b. Love your child for who she is, not what she does or doesn't do
   c. Don't withdraw love as a punishment or hand it out as a reward
2. ACCEPT EACH CHILD FOR WHO HE IS
   a. Understand that each child is unique
   b. Imagine how things look from your child's point of view
   c. *Accept* doesn't mean "agree"

PARENTING PILLAR #3: NURTURING AND EMPOWERING ENCOURAGEMENT

When I was growing up, my parents had a plaque hanging on the wall in our family room that read "Roots and Wings." It was the philosophy they lived by in parenting their four young boys, and to me it is infinitely profound. Giving your child a strong, safe foundation from which she can fly is something we should all aspire to do as parents. Unconditional Love and Acceptance will undoubtedly give your child roots. To give them wings, I recommend Nurturing and Empowering Encouragement. This will allow your child the room to discover, problem solve, and ultimately develop independence.

Another quote I love is by author Sloan Wilson and says, "The hardest part of raising children is teaching them to ride bicycles. A shaky child on a bicycle for the first time needs both support and freedom. The realization that this is what the child will always need can hit hard."[4] This is scary, I know. It's hard to let our children fly without always wanting to be right there with a safety net. But if you've given your child the roots of Unconditional Love and Acceptance and you encourage him in a way that is both Nurturing and Empowering, you'll find that he will spread his wings and develop into a mature, confident human being.

As you know, children are innately curious. They love to explore and discover. By encouraging your child in a manner that is both nurturing and lovingly supportive, yet is also empowering them with their own sense of independence, you are doing wonders for their development as a lifelong explorer and learner.

So how exactly do you find the balance between Nurturing and Empowering? Sway one way and you become smothering; sway the other and you become aloof. The first step is to *Cultivate a Nurturing and Supportive Environment*. My martial arts classes are renowned for the atmosphere they create for the children. It is a safe, supportive environment that allows for trial and error. Children are encouraged to do their best, instead of comparing themselves to others. They are challenged to grow, and they always feel safe to make a mistake. By not feeling afraid of making mistakes, children take the chance to stretch to their full potential. Any feelings of fear or insecurity are addressed in a nurturing manner so that children learn that although these feelings are normal, they don't need to be ruled by them.

Once you've cultivated a nurturing, supportive environment, step two is to *Offer Empowering Encouragement*. It's a great idea to continuously offer your child age-appropriate positive choices. Children feel empowered when they can make decisions that affect their lives. By offering your child choices, you are giving her your respect, building her confidence, and helping her learn to make judgments and decisions. Of course, the choices need to be limited and age appropriate. For example, you might ask your toddler whether she wants to wear the red shirt or the blue shirt. You might ask a third grader whether he wants to go to the zoo or to the park. If you are planning a family vacation and find two or three hotels that are equally agreeable to you, present the options to your eighth grader and ask her to choose. That child will feel very proud for making a decision for the entire family.

When offering choices, don't leave them open-ended; make sure the options are always positive, and be sure your child won't feel he disappointed you with his choice. You wouldn't want to give the message that your child made the wrong choice. This would undermine the whole purpose of giving him or her an option.

Besides offering choices, another great way to *Offer Empowering Encouragement* is to entrust your child with age-appropriate and achievable responsibilities. Giving your child responsibility will give her the message that you think she is worthy and capable of making positive contributions. Austrian psychologist Alfred Adler (1870–1937) was a pioneer in shifting the perspective of parents from the "children should be seen and not heard" philosophy to one that espouses that children deserve to be treated with dignity and respect. He believed that once a child's basic needs for food, shelter, and safety are met, her primary emotional goal is to achieve a sense of belonging and significance. Entrusting your child with age-appropriate and achievable responsibilities develops a feeling of belonging: your child knows she is making a contribution, and she feels a sense of significance because her actions are meaningful and valuable. You may give your child regular chores, but try to also offer him empowering responsibilities that don't feel like required chores.

For example, ask your young child to be responsible for crossing off items from the shopping list while at the grocery store. If your child is able to do the math, ask for his help in doubling a recipe. Let your child dress himself if he is old enough to physically do so.

It's often hard not to jump in and automatically do things for your child, either because you want to help her or because you are feeling a time crunch and expediency has unconsciously become your top priority. However, children will not learn to feel capable and responsible if an adult always interferes. So another key element to Nurturing and Empowering Encouragement is to allow your child to do what she can before offering help. Rudolf Dreikurs, MD, (1897–1972), a protégé of Alfred Adler's, translated Adler's theory into practical parenting tips and good advice for parents. He often said, "Don't do anything for a child that a child can do for herself." If we do, we are sending the message that we don't think she is capable, that she needs to be taken care of, and that she is entitled to your constant care and attention. Dependent children often become demanding children. But giving your child the chance to do what she can before you offer assistance is very empowering, and if your child feels safe in knowing that you are available to step in, she will feel nurtured and not afraid to try new things.

So remember to help your child spread his wings by giving him Nurturing and Empowering Encouragement—encourage your child to be his best instead of comparing himself to others; support your child in learning from his mistakes; entrust your child with age-appropriate choices and responsibilities; and allow your child to do what he can before offering your help.

Support and Freedom. Roots and Wings. Once you get the hang of it, it's a beautiful prescription for parenting your child.

PARENTING PILLAR #3— NURTURING AND EMPOWERING ENCOURAGEMENT

1. CULTIVATE A NURTURING AND SUPPORTIVE ENVIRONMENT
   a. Encourage your child to be his best instead of comparing himself to others
   b. Support your child in learning from his mistakes
2. OFFER EMPOWERING ENCOURAGEMENT
   a. Entrust your child with age-appropriate choices and responsibilites
   b. Allow your child to do what she can before offering help

---

PARENTING PILLAR #4: EMPOWERING DISCIPLINE

By now you know that the basis for the Life Ki-do Tools for Life system is about empowering children with tools to help them look inward instead of looking outward to others for their validation and sense of self. We have seen that this intrinsically based approach will give children more control of their own lives, which develops confidence and self-worth and ultimately more happiness and fulfillment. So naturally my approach to discipline is also one that is based on educating and empowering the child instead of shaming and blaming.

Many approaches to discipline are based on an extrinsic model where the child's behavior is predominantly monitored by an outside source—parent or teacher. In this model, the adult usually doles out rewards and punishment as a means of motivating the child to behave in a certain way. If you've tried this type of discipline, you may have found it sometimes works in the short-term to stop misbehavior or to encourage "good" behavior. Although there might be an immediate correction to the misbehavior, there are often long-term negative effects of this type of discipline. I love the statement from Jane Nelsen, author of *Positive Discipline*, "Where did we ever get the crazy idea that in order to make children DO better, first we have to make them FEEL worse."[5]

The major flaw with punishment is that instead of a child learning to do the right thing for the right reasons from her own intrinsic motivation, she is going through the motions of good behavior out of fear of punishment or temptation of a reward. Instead of inspiring self-reflection and an intrinsic desire to make better choices, punishments can leave the child feeling angry, defensive, and primed for a power struggle, or hurt, shamed, and overly fixated on pleasing others. This approach leaves a weak foundation for the child to make good decisions on her own in the future.

For example, one traditional approach to teaching martial arts uses intimidation and humiliation as a teaching methodology. Student performance is based on trying to please the sensei and avoid punishment. In the classes at Life Ki-do Academy, however, the environment is based on mutual respect, and the children are encouraged to perform well to please themselves instead of pleasing the instructors. There is great emphasis for the children to find their own strength and motivation, which is something they can easily transfer to other aspects of their lives.

Also, when a child is punished, it is very common for him to feel overwhelmed and consumed by his negative emotions and then associate those negative emotions with the person giving the punishment (namely you!). If this is a common practice in your home, the child will perceive your relationship more as a dictatorship based on control rather than a relationship based on mutual respect.

I have worked with a wide spectrum of behavior issues in my years as a sensei, and I know there are times when you as the adult are at your wit's end and just need immediate results. But in my experience, Empowering Discipline will not only yield the results you want but will also develop a healthy and enjoyable long-term relationship between you and your child. And from the modeling of this healthy parent-child relationship, your child will then learn to treat other people with care and respect. Furthermore, your child will feel empowered rather than shamed, which will fertilize her confidence and develop her autonomy.

The first step to Empowering Discipline is to *Create a Team Approach* where children are respected as individuals and invited to be active participants in the family unit. When parents and children walk through the doors of my academy, they immediately feel the mutual respect of the team approach. Of course, there is structure, and I am still the teacher. I give instruction. I guide the children. I am leading them. But I am also respecting them. I am asking for their input. I am working with them instead of standing above them. It is a doing *with* instead of doing *to*. This same philosophy is highly effective in the family unit as well.

Once you've created a team approach, of course you want to know what to do in the heat of the moment. How do you apply Empowering Discipline in the midst of tension, frustration, anger, or exhaustion? Before you address the child, you need to first address yourself—I call this *Ground and Connect*.

The first step to *Ground and Connect* in an escalated situation with your child is to breathe. I am fortunate to have trained with world-renowned Russian martial arts instructors who are masters at using the breath to deal with fear, pain, and survival. If the breath can help them in a do-or-die situation, it can surely help when you are in the trenches with your own little warrior. So take a "Time-in" for yourself by doing some *Ninja Breathing*. You can see chapter 3 for more details, but basically *Ninja Breathing* is slow and deep breathing in through the nose and out through the mouth. If your child is safe and you feel that you need to remove yourself from the tense situation for a few minutes, then by all means do so. Regardless, by taking a few deep breaths to calm and center yourself, you will be better prepared to address the situation. Calming and centering yourself will serve to help calm your child as you model the use of *Ninja Breathing* in a challenging situation.

The opposite is also true. Of course, it's normal that your first reaction to misbehavior might be anger or frustration. But if you try to address the behavioral issue while in this heightened emotional state, you will only add more upset to the situation. Think of a time in your own life when you have made a mistake or lacked good judgment. If someone immediately approached you with intense emotions of anger or frustration, you most likely became defensive or shut down rather than opening up to address the situation.

For example, one of my students I'll call Sally asked her mom one day if she could have a sleepover at a friend's house. Sally's mom told me that when she said no and tried to explain why, Sally threw a tantrum, saying she wished she had a "cool" mom like her friend did. She ran to her room and slammed the door. The immediate reaction for Sally's mom was hurt masked by anger. She opened Sally's door, and with resentment and disdain in her voice, she began to reprimand Sally for speaking to her like that. Now both were in a heightened emotional state that left little room for resolution. In that moment, Sally's mom said she remembered to *Ground and Connect* by taking a few deep *Ninja Breaths*. She said it took just a few moments to calm and center herself, thus becoming able to connect with her daughter and address the situation.

The next part to *Ground and Connect* is to accept the current situation. Resisting will only increase your frustration level. It is what it is, and the sooner you can accept the situation, the easier it will be for you to look beyond your primal emotional responses to find a more clear and level-headed approach. Finally, try to connect to the child, not his behavior. Remember that while your child always needs your Unconditional Love and Acceptance, accepting doesn't mean agreeing. You can disapprove of your child's specific behavior without rejecting the whole child.

After you've taken time, whether that be one minute or one day, to *Ground and Connect*, the next step is to *Reflect and Resolve*. The goal of reflection is to help the child become aware of and understand the root of the misbehavior. First, reflect on your child's behavior. Then ask the child for her perspective on the behavior. A team approach, remember? Usually misbehavior is a symptom of some deeper issue. So really look, listen, and feel what might be behind the behavior. Remember that psychologist Alfred Adler said that a child's primary emotional goal is to achieve a sense of belonging (strong positive relationships with others; feeling connected to family, friends, and peers) and significance (a strong positive sense of self; feeling capable, worthy and empowered). Look behind the misbehavior to see if it's a result of the child not feeling one of these two things.

After you have taken a moment to reflect (and I know sometimes you might have just a moment before needing to step in!), then you can ask the child for her perspective. This offers respect to the child and allows her to feel part of the team. You'll be surprised how insightful children can be, and asking them to reflect on their own behavior will develop their muscles to self-regulate in the future. Even if you are angry or frustrated, it's important to ask them questions with a tone of genuine respect for what they have to say. Try to withhold your own judgment here. It's truly an important experience for the child to learn to monitor her behavior intrinsically rather than extrinsically.

For example, I was working in a fourth-grade classroom one day when a temper tantrum erupted and a boy turned his classmate's desk into a dump truck, dumping all his belongings on the floor. A normal course of action would be to immediately punish the boy so that he would know his actions were not tolerated. However, I asked the boy whether he would step aside with me for a moment. I asked him if he could rewind and tell me what happened right before he threw everything on the floor. The boy said that they were taking a test and his classmate was tapping the back of his chair with his foot. I asked him to rewind even further to see how he was feeling during the test before the boy began kicking his chair. He looked down solemnly and said that the test was too hard and he didn't know how to answer the questions. I asked him how it made him feel to not know the answers. He was quickly able to identify that he felt sad, frustrated, and not smart enough. I then helped him connect those feelings with his misbehavior so that he could understand the root of what happened. The lesson learned here was that the boy realized the situation was not solely about his classmate's tapping; it was about his own deeper feelings of not being good enough (significance) and not feeling connected with his classmates (belonging). This realization allowed him to offer a genuine apology rather than an empty one that was merely part of the prescription for punishment. It also taught him that he could be more responsible for his feelings rather than blaming others. Instead of getting stuck in a typical cycle of not feeling good about himself/misbehaving/being punished, this boy was offered a chance to feel empowered and break the vicious cycle.

Sometimes in the reflection process, a child may have difficulty identifying the feelings behind his misbehavior. So it may be helpful for you to make an observation about his emotional state. For example, you can say, "You seem frustrated," or "I'm not sure how you feel, but if I was in that situation I might be feeling sad." The child might then be able to relate to the feeling you have identified and connect that feeling to the misbehavior. If your observation was correct, the child will probably feel understood and thus more open to discussing the behavior. However, even if you wrongly label the emotion, it may provoke the child to say, "No, that's not how I'm feeling, I'm actually feeling x." This can still spark a good discussion about what's really behind the misbehavior.

Once you have both had a chance to *Reflect*, it's time to work on a solution to *Resolve* the situation. It's critical here for the child not to feel shamed but rather to feel included in a solution. If you focus on solutions together instead of immediately issuing a punishment, you are inviting the child to become part of her own personal development. Finally, it's great to wrap it up by asking your child how she could better deal with the situation if it was to happen again in the future.

Empowering Discipline is often put to the test on my martial arts mats. One particular day two boys, I'll call them Sam and Max, were wrestling when Sam lost it. He lost control both emotionally and physically and started screaming and really hitting out hard at Max. My assistant instructor jumped right in and was able to stop the misbehavior and make sure both boys were safe. The whole room—the other students, the parents watching, and yes, even I—was shaken from the intensity.

Because I had already laid the foundation for a *Team Approach*, I knew the first step was to *Ground and Connect* everyone in the room. I asked the entire class, including the two boys, the parents, the assistant instructor, and myself, to sit down and take some *Ninja Breaths* together. I knew it was important not to shame Sam by sending him to a corner or having him do push-ups on his own. This boy was obviously upset, and the last thing he needed was more blame and shame dumped on him. But he did need to understand that his behavior was unacceptable and that he needed to take responsibility for it. I knew we needed to *Reflect and Resolve*, so I used the fourth Tool for Life— My Shoes, Your Shoes, Our Shoes—with the two boys. We'll learn more about that tool in chapter 6, but the point here is that both boys had a chance to speak, be heard, and come to an understanding.

It was amazing how honest and forthcoming both boys were about their actions and the feelings behind them. Both boys were willing to take responsibility for their part in the situation, make an effort to understand the other's perspective, and give their feedback about how in the future they could better deal with their respective emotions. I then asked the boys if they needed more time for *Ninja Breathing* or if they could continue wrestling this time as friends. Both made the choice to continue wrestling as friends, and they did so amicably and with resolution and even some lighthearted laughter. It was a powerful lesson for everyone involved. If there had been only a swift punishment issued for Sam, not only would he have left the situation feeling worse than he was already feeling, but there would have been no room for understanding his behavior and the feelings behind it. Not only would he have failed to grow from the experience, but most likely he would have ended up repeating the same behavior.

I hope you can see that instead of issuing a punishment that shames and blames the child, Empowering Discipline gives the child an opportunity to be aware of what caused the behavior, take responsibility to remedy the situation, and be prepared to better deal with a similar situation if it should arise again.

PARENTING PILLAR #4— EMPOWERING DISCIPLINE

1. CREATE A TEAM APPROACH
   a. Respect your child as an individual
   b. Invite your child to be an active participant in the family unit
2. GROUND AND CONNECT
   a. Breathe and take a "Time-In"
   b. Accept the current situation
   c. Connect to the child, not the behavior
3. REFLECT AND RESOLVE
   a. Look, listen, and feel what may be behind the behavior
   b. Ask the child for her perspective on the behavior
   c. Involve the child in coming up with a solution

PARENTING PILLARS SUMMARY

PARENTING PILLAR #1— MODELING

1. BE GENUINE
   a. Your words are congruent with your feelings
   b. Your actions are congruent with your words
2. GET PERSONAL
   a. Share your successes and challenges
   b. Be age appropriate

PARENTING PILLAR #2— UNCONDITIONAL LOVE & ACCEPTANCE

1. GIVE UNCONDITIONAL LOVE
   a. Listen and speak to your child with love and respect
   b. Love your child for who she is, not what she does or doesn't do
   c. Don't withdraw love as a punishment or hand it out as a reward
2. ACCEPT EACH CHILD FOR WHO HE IS
   a. Understand that each child is unique
   b. Imagine how things look from your child's point of view
   c. *Accept* doesn't mean "agree"

PARENTING PILLAR #3—
NURTURING AND EMPOWERING ENCOURAGEMENT

1. CULTIVATE A NURTURING AND SUPPORTIVE ENVIRONMENT
   a. Encourage your child to be his best instead of comparing himself to others
   b. Support your child in learning from his mistakes
2. OFFER EMPOWERING ENCOURAGEMENT
   a. Entrust your child with age-appropriate choices and responsibilites
   b. Allow your child to do what she can before offering help

PARENTING PILLAR #4—
EMPOWERING DISCIPLINE

1. CREATE A TEAM APPROACH
   a. Respect your child as an individual
   b. Invite your child to be an active participant in the family unit
2. GROUND AND CONNECT
   a. Breathe and take a "Time-In"
   b. Accept the current situation
   c. Connect to the child, not the behavior
3. REFLECT AND RESOLVE
   a. Look, listen, and feel what may be behind the behavior
   b. Ask the child for her perspective on the behavior
   c. Involve the child in coming up with a solution

CHAPTER 3

TOOL #1: RIVER CHECK-IN FOR FOCUS AND MINDFULNESS

The faculty of voluntarily bringing back a wandering attention, over and over again, is the very root of judgment, character, and will . . . An education which should improve this faculty would be the education par excellence.

—*William James, 1890*

On your mark. Get set. Go! Many of us can probably remember being in PE class and starting a race via those words. Ever feel that same way when you wake up in the morning? Sometimes life can feel like a race, and unfortunately with that often comes anxiety and a feeling of being unprepared or overwhelmed. To combat those feelings, I believe the starting point to anything in life is to be mentally, emotionally, and physically present, strong, and fluid. But how do we learn how to do that?

In most martial arts, one is usually taught a ready stance, which is similar to being on your mark in a race. A ready stance prescribes a very specific placement of the arms and feet, sometimes down to a matter of degrees and inches. However, depending on whether you are learning karate, tae kwon do, aikido, judo, etc., the ready stance may vary. So although these ready stances are very good at preparing you for a specific type of attack or defense, they are not fluid enough to be effective for all types of situations.

However, due to the complexity and diversity of their country's terrain as well as the varied styles and weapons of their attackers, the Russians needed to be physically, mentally, and emotionally prepared for any possible situation. So they developed Systema, a martial arts style free of a set stance, strict rules, and rigid structure but that allowed soldiers to prepare with their individual strengths and instinctive reactions. I adapted some of the main principles of Systema (breath, posture, relaxation, and movement) for the first Tool for Life to help prepare Life Ki-do students to thrive within the complexity of daily living.

Being present and focusing on the task at hand is really the starting point to accomplish anything in life. River Check-in helps children not only to focus but also to monitor their mental, physical, and emotional states with the strength and fluidity of a Russian warrior. By doing a River Check-in using the 3 Bs (Body, Breath, and Brain), the child can easily assess her current state and make adjustments as needed. It is an empowering and tangible tool that makes it easy for even young children to self-regulate. (Hint: More self-regulation by your child means less micromanaging aka nagging by you and overall fewer power struggles.) To make it simple for children to understand, we say that River Check-in helps you to focus on what you are doing.

A BACKGROUND IN MINDFULNESS

For thousands of years, both spiritual monks and martial arts warriors practiced what we today call mindfulness. In the past twenty-five years, interest in mindfulness has soared. Hundreds of clinical research studies and mindfulness-based programs have been developed to help people with a variety of psychological, physical, and interpersonal issues. Many books have been written on the subject, and popular media regularly reports on the benefits of mindfulness, including increased executive attention, behavioral regulation, and self-control.

What exactly is mindfulness? Simply, mindfulness is a clear awareness of your inner and outer world at any given moment. Your inner world is your thoughts, feelings, emotions, and sensations, and your outer world is your actions and surroundings. Clear awareness means that you are being objective without judging, labeling, or comparing based on your ideas or opinions from your past experiences. Rather, you are simply noticing what is taking place. In its fullest expression, mindfulness involves the fluid self-regulation of states of attention and awareness.[1]

In Life Ki-do training, our goal is to be always fluid, like a River—not too tight like Ice or too loose like a Puddle. So in regard to being focused or mindful, a River Check-in helps children to be aware of their current state but also to be able to self-regulate and adjust their state to come back to a place of emotional and mental balance. To a state of relaxed focus and presence. To being strong yet fluid like a River—the perfect way to live.

RIVER CHECK-IN WITH THE 3 Bs— BODY, BREATH, AND BRAIN

Parents and teachers so often tell children to "pay attention," and as adults we have all heard "to be in the moment." But how do we "pay attention" or "be in the moment"? To help children find a state of relaxed focus and presence, I created the River Check-in. To make it simple and easy to remember, the River Check-in asks children to check in and regulate their 3 Bs, namely Body, Breath, and Brain.

Think of a time when you felt nervous, scared, or angry. Did your heart rate increase? Did you start perspiring more? What was your breathing like? Most likely in times of emotional upset, your body and breath were also affected. Or think of a time when your body was physically hurt—maybe you burned yourself on the stove or twisted an ankle playing a game of one-on-one. When you felt that physical pain, what happened in your brain? How was your breathing affected? Did other muscles in your body tense up?

Remember that song "Dry Bones" that goes something like, "With the leg bone connected to the knee bone, and the knee bone connected to the thigh bone, and the thigh bone connected to the hip bone . . ."? The 3 Bs are something like that. The Body, Breath, and Brain are closely connected to one another. I tell children that the 3 Bs are really good friends and that any time one of the Bs does something, it affects the other two Bs.

Whether you are a warrior on the battlefield or a child on the soccer field, River Check-in with the 3 Bs is a great tool to master. I have seen teachers in the classroom ask children to check their 3 Bs before starting a new lesson. It's much more effective than yelling out to pay attention. I've received feedback from parents that they find it helpful to do a River Check-in with their child before he starts homework in order to set a quiet, focused tone. And I've heard from quite a few students that they practice their 3 Bs when feeling anxious or stressed during those dreaded standardized tests. The applications are endless, and the more your child practices the 3 Bs, the more he will be able to tap into the benefits and the connection between the three.

B #1—BODY CHECK

Having a strong and fluid body enhances the ability to focus and be mindful. Body Check is the first B because it is the most tangible, and it is the easiest for children to be aware of and to adjust. In a Body Check, we specifically look at posture and muscle tension. Both of these components have a direct correlation to higher body and brain function and our ability to focus.

Quite often when we think of being focused, we think our bodies need to be overly tense, rigid, and hyperalert. In fact, some sports and certain martial arts styles encourage that kind of tense focus. However, in Life Ki-do Martial Arts we believe that any unnecessary tension will lead to long-term stress and possibly injury to the body. So once again we find ourselves back at the River that encourages both strength and fluidity.

Kayley, one of my kindergarten students, illustrated that a Body Check can be useful in any daily situation. She told me one day that when she had been eating her breakfast that morning she performed a Body Check and noticed that she was hunching over while eating her cereal. Of course, eating her cereal didn't require Kayley's utmost attention and focus, yet she wanted to be more mindful and present. Her smile and exuberance while telling me her story told me how much better she felt after doing her Body Check. This little five-year-old was so proud of herself, and she felt empowered because she had the tools to take care of herself.

STEPS TO BODY CHECK

1. Spine: Long and strong
2. Muscles: Not too tight, not too loose, but in the middle like a river

. . .

Step 1—Spine: Long and Strong

The first element to the Body Check is the spine. We ask children to make sure their spines are long and strong, like Kayley did while eating her cereal. This step encourages a good, upright, and balanced posture in which all the body segments are balanced and in optimal alignment, whether one is stationary (sitting or standing) or in motion (daily action, sports, or exercise).

"Sit up straight!" "Don't slouch!" Somehow these phrases always end up in a mom's vocabulary. However, those words can provoke a child to be like Ice with a spine that is too rigid or too tense. This kind of posture can create feelings of nervousness, irritation, anger, or stress. Using too much muscle strength in a rigid posture means energy is being wasted on the body instead of being available to the brain.

On the other hand, posture that is too much like a Puddle with a spine that is hunched or slouched can make a child apathetic, lazy, or disengaged. In this case, the body's ligaments, muscles, and tendons are struggling to keep the body in balance, causing fatigue. Also, in this kind of slouched position the lungs are squashed, restricting air flow, which makes the brain more tired and slow to react and think.

By asking your child to check his body for a long and strong spine, you are asking him to check that his alignment and posture are not too rigid or too loose. When the spine is long and strong, your child's bones and joints are in correct alignment, and his muscles can be used more efficiently. Thus the body requires less energy to move about. This decreases fatigue and allows more energy to be available for the brain and focus.

A long, strong spine also allows for the lungs to fully expand. Fuller, deeper breaths allow more oxygen to be inhaled, which then allows the brain to function more effectively. When the brain functions effectively, cognitive abilities, concentration, and focus levels are increased.

Step 2 — Muscles: Not Too Tight, Not Too Loose, but in the Middle like a River

The second step in the Body Check is to make sure the muscles are not too tight like Ice and not too loose like a Puddle but in the middle like a River. By using the analogies of Ice, Puddle, and River, children can find a balance between tension and relaxation to find the optimal state to be present, focused, and mindful.

Imagine trying to soak up a spill with a sponge that is being squeezed. Muscles that are too tight are the same—they don't allow much blood to pass through, decreasing blood circulation. This can lead to lack of focus and concentration as well as overall fatigue. Overly tense muscles can also cause shallow breathing, creating more body tension and stress to the mind.

On the other hand, a body with muscles too loose like a Puddle doesn't have the alertness and strength for focus and concentration. Without strong muscle tone, oxygen is not being effectively circulated to the brain.

However, if the muscles are in the middle, both strong and relaxed like a River, blood flow is increased. An increase in circulation brings energy-producing nutrients and oxygen to the cells of the body and carries away metabolic waste products that can make one feel listless and drained.

A focus game I like to play with children, based on exercises from the Russian martial art Systema, is to ask them to consciously tense and relax their muscles. The point of this game is twofold. It not only strengthens focus, but it gives children the awareness of what it feels like to have muscles overly tense or overly relaxed. You can try this at home with your child. One way to play this game is to ask your child to squeeze her entire body while inhaling and then to fully relax her entire body while exhaling. While she is tightening her muscles, it may be helpful if you encourage her with your voice, saying, "Squeeze! Squeeze! Squeeze!" or "Tight, Tight, Tight." Then while she is relaxing her muscles, you can encourage her to completely let go by modeling a big exhale.

Another way to play this game is to ask your child to squeeze and relax individual body parts, such as arms, legs, or torso. For example, you can ask your child to tighten and squeeze his left leg while inhaling and then to release the tension with a big, slow exhale. Then ask him to tighten his right arm while inhaling and then to release with another big, slow exhale. Keep going until you see that your child is more relaxed and focused.

In general, this game is effective in helping children focus, settle down, and develop body awareness. There are many layers to this exercise that go beyond the scope of this book, but just have fun and be creative coming up with different combinations. The combination and order of tensing and relaxing muscles is not important; just be sure to ask your child to inhale while tensing and exhale while letting go.

B #2—BREATH CHECK

The second step in the River Check-in is a Breath Check. The Breath, the second of the three Bs, has always played a major role in the training I do with my martial arts students. I have consistently heard overwhelming feedback from parents and students about the positive benefits of the breath work outside of our dojo. They are not alone in their observations. The American Medical Student Association says, "Using and learning proper breathing techniques is one of the most beneficial things that can be done for both short- and long-term physical and emotional health."[2]

Amazingly, breathing is the one internal system that we are able to consciously regulate. It is the only bodily function that we do both voluntarily and involuntarily. Breathing exercises can act as a bridge into those functions of the body for which we generally do not have conscious control, such as blood pressure, heart rate, circulation, and digestion. Dr. Andrew Newberg says, "Research has shown that breathing exercises lower stress and anxiety, improve coping skills, help people deal with substance abuse, improve their general sense of well-being, and improve self-esteem. Breathing exercises also help people deal with problems such as panic disorder, heart disease, and lung disease."[3]

Think of how you might unconsciously use your breath. Under stress or fear we often hold our breath, which restricts blood flow to the brain and can cause us to freeze or panic. If we are afraid, sad, or angry, our breath can become short, choppy, or too forced. This adversely affects our brain function and our ability to respond and react efficiently and appropriately. If we feel relief from stress, we often take a deep breath or sigh. This is our body's natural response to wanting to take in more oxygen after having deprived itself with short and fearful breaths.

So we know that at times our emotional or physical state has an unconscious effect on our breath, but how about turning that around and using our breath to have a conscious effect on our brain and body? Teaching your child the secrets of how to consciously use her breath is truly giving her a gift that will last a lifetime. The breath is something we often take for granted, but if your child learns to harness its tremendous power, she will reap great benefits. When children learn how to use their breath as youngsters, it really becomes second nature to them, and they will naturally use it when feeling unfocused, scared, overwhelmed, anxious, nervous, or angry.

I have seen this with children as young as preschoolers. Alex, one of our three-year-old students, fell off a swing and broke his arm. When the paramedics arrived they told Alex's mom that she could ride with him to the hospital but that they were not allowed to take her five-year-old daughter in the ambulance. Not able to leave her daughter with anyone, Alex's mom had no choice but to leave three-year-old Alex alone with the paramedics on the ride to the hospital. She was distraught, but she glanced at Alex lying on the gurney holding his arm, and she saw that he was quietly doing the breathing he had learned in his Life Ki-do classes. She was stunned and couldn't believe her little boy had such bravery and strength to deal with this physically and emotionally difficult time. The whole scene was very scary, and Alex's mom was grateful that the breathing technique Alex had learned was such a natural and immediate response for her little one.

There are many different types and patterns of breathing exercises and mindful awareness practices used across martial arts. For now, we'll focus on just three types of breathing: *Ninja Breathing* for times of stress or anxiety, *Fire Breathing* for awakening and focusing the brain, and *River Breathing* for everyday awareness and mindfulness.

STEPS TO BREATH CHECK

1. Ninja Breathing: To calm and de-stress

2. Fire Breathing: To energize and focus

3. River Breathing: To focus and feel good

Step 1—Ninja Breathing: To Calm and De-stress
(Slow, deep breaths in the nose and out the mouth)

I have been teaching *Ninja Breathing* to children for almost twenty years, and it is honestly one of the most powerful and empowering tools that I teach. I have heard countless stories of children using *Ninja Breathing* on their own or with a suggestion from a parent in times of emotional or physical pain in a wide variety of scenarios, from bad dreams to bike accidents, from focus issues in the classroom to feeling left out on the playground.

To help children understand the importance and impact of *Ninja Breathing,* I explain that this type of breathing has been used by warriors and wise men throughout time in order to feel stronger on their insides and to deal with any fear or pain. I explain to my students that they can get the same great benefits from *Ninja Breathing* in their life today. Of course, the word *ninja* gives them the sense that they will be getting special powers from this kind of breathing.

Ninja Breathing is very simple—it's just a slow inhale through the nose and a slow, deep exhale through the mouth. The breath should come deep from the belly, expanding the belly on the inhale and contracting the belly on the exhale. To help your child remember to breathe deeply, you can ask him to rest one of his hands on his belly and make sure that he sees his hand rise on the inhale and fall with the exhale. Because children often want to suck in their belly on the inhale, it is often easier if you tell them to first exhale and pull the belly in. Then proceed to the inhale and expanding the belly. Another thing to be careful of is that children often exaggerate the inhale to make sure they are getting it right. They can have a tendency to raise their shoulders or make their muscles overly tight when inhaling. This creates added tension and stress and so should be avoided.

Deep belly breathing will help your child's chest expand to its full potential, pulling air into the lower lobes of the lungs where the greatest amount of blood flow occurs. This occurs because deep abdominal breathing pushes downward on the diaphragm, the muscle between the chest and abdomen, causing the abdomen to expand and creating a negative pressure within the chest, which forces air into the lungs. This negative pressure pulls blood into the chest and heart, leading to improved stamina. In addition, the slow belly breathing in *Ninja Breathing* stimulates the parasympathetic nervous system, which controls the body's relaxation response, helping to harmonize the nervous system and calm and de-stress the mind.

A five-year-old kindergarten student in one of my martial arts classes found *Ninja Breathing* so helpful that she decided to use the technique to help fellow students at her academic school. She created the *Ninja Breathing* Ambulance. Anytime that someone was hurt on the playground, she and a few other friends would pull up in their *Ninja Breathing* Ambulance and they would all do their breathing together. This is the kind of magic that can happen when you empower a child.

In another instance of students helping others with *Ninja Breathing*, Kyle, one of my eight-year-old students, told me that he and two friends were playing a ball game at recess when the other two boys ran into each other. One boy had a bloody face and the other had a bloody elbow. Kyle started doing his *Ninja Breathing* and suggested that his friends join him. The three of them sat together doing *Ninja Breathing* and then wiped themselves off and continued playing. After telling me this story, Kyle gave me a wise look and said, "Breathing really works. Basically, *Ninja Breathing* has changed my life. Actually, *Ninja Breathing* has *majorly* changed my life." For a boy with focus issues and emotional challenges, this was a profound shift that exemplified his newfound confidence and inner strength.

 ## Step 2—Fire Breathing: To Energize and Focus
(Fast, short breaths in the nose and out the nose)

While *Ninja Breathing* helps children be calm and less like Ice, *Fire Breathing* helps them to energize and be less like a Puddle. Similar to the yogic Breath of Fire, in *Fire Breathing* both the inhale and exhale are through the nose, and the breaths are quick, short, and sharp. Short, fast rhythmic breaths increase energy in the brain and body by releasing energizing chemicals such as epinephrine, also known as adrenaline. This type of breathing mimics the chest breathing we do when under stress and thus stimulates the adrenal glands to make us aware and alert. *Fire Breathing* is effective for short bursts but shouldn't be done for extended periods of time.

To make *Fire Breathing* fun for children, I often tell them to imagine a laser right in the middle of their forehead. This laser will focus and wake up their brain. Then I tell them to breathe fast in and out their nose and imagine that these breaths are the jet fuel the laser needs to wake up the brain. Try it right now for yourself and see whether you feel more awake after just a few moments. *Fire Breathing* is a great technique to use anytime your child needs a quick boost of energy, and it's much healthier than a sugar high!

Step 3—River Breathing: To Focus and Feel Good
(Slow, deep breaths in the nose and out the nose)

If a child doesn't need to be calmed or energized, then *River Breathing* is the most appropriate technique for focusing and feeling good. The quality of breathing is like a River. It is deep and even from the belly, and the breath is in and out through the nose. Slow, focused breathing such as this will trigger the body's natural relaxation response and also increase dopamine levels in different parts of the brain. Dopamine is a neurotransmitter that helps control the brain's reward and pleasure centers, which is why this kind of breathing creates both a pleasurable and calm experience. In addition, the focused nasal breathing of *River Breathing* increases the release of nitric oxide in the body, which improves the functioning of the lungs and circulatory system. Increased nitric oxide can also assist in the lowering of anxiety, especially in socially intense situations.[4]

River Breathing should be like a pendulum swinging back and forth evenly and rhythmically. At the end of each inhale you feel more energy, and at the end of each exhale you feel more relaxation. The continuity of those two is just like nature's rhythm of a wave in the ocean going in and out. The longer your child can practice the steady rhythm of *River Breathing*, the more her thoughts and emotions will settle down, and the more focused and aware she will be.

One of my nine-year-old students told me that he struggled with and feared those very long annual standardized tests. However, after learning how to do a Breath Check, he was happy to report that he practiced all three breathing techniques throughout the testing period and was able to stay calm, focused, and on task over the three days. He told me that in the car ride to school and at the beginning of the test, he used his *Ninja Breathing* to calm and relax his nerves. Then he switched to *River Breathing* to keep himself focused and fluid during the test. When he caught his brain feeling tired and distracted, he quietly practiced his *Fire Breathing* to give him an energy and focus boost. When telling me this story, he looked really proud of himself and was happy and relieved that he had real tools to be successful. I have no doubt that he will apply these breathing techniques to many other areas of his life, and as someone who reaps the benefits of doing Breath Checks as an adult, I truly wish I had had the same opportunity when I was a child. It is my passion to empower as many children as possible with the great gift of the breath.

B #3 — BRAIN CHECK

The third and final step in the River Check-in is the Brain Check. Just as for the Body and the Breath, the optimal state for the Brain is to be both strong and fluid—that is, both focused and calm. However, without some kind of regulation, our poor brains are constantly bombarded with our thoughts and it's very difficult to focus. Our thoughts can be like pinballs in the brain—scattered and chaotic.

The irony is that as amazing and evolved as the human brain is, the brain is also fertile ground for our suffering. Only we humans worry about the future, regret the past, and blame ourselves for the present. And unfortunately, we spend so much of our time thinking about the past or the future that we miss the fulfillment that comes from truly living in the moment.

So it's helpful to be aware of some of the brain's tricks and limitations in order to learn to use it more effectively. For example, it's good to know that the brain will actually fabricate stories to fill in details for events that have happened in the past or for things yet to happen in the future. So don't always believe everything your mind is telling you! Also, while it's great that our frontal lobes are more evolved than those of other mammals, giving us the capability to plan and strategize about the future, this great ability often leads to great anxiety. Do you ever see your dog or cat anxious or stressed about the future?

Another trick of the brain is that, for survival purposes, our brains prioritize negative information instead of positive information. This means we usually pay much more attention to criticism than praise, and that we are generally more attentive to the bad things that happen in life rather than the good. (Isn't it obvious that the news media is aware of this tendency?) Research has shown that people experience more negative emotion if they lose $100 than positive emotion if they win $100.

So with an overabundance of external stimuli and a brain that is constantly making choices about what information to delete, what to pay attention to, and what to fill in, how do we reel it all in? Focusing the brain does take training, but with consistent practice it becomes easier. I tell children that the brain is just like a muscle in the body that needs exercise to become stronger. In fact, that's exactly how it works. There are neural pathways in our brain and when we fire the same neurons again and again, consciously directing our attention with focus and awareness, we are making those pathways stronger. Using the mind to change the brain is called self-directed neuroplasticity.

You most likely don't see yourself discussing the science of self-directed neuroplasticity with your child. So to make this technique kid-friendly, we simply call it a Brain Check. A Brain Check gives children tangible steps to strengthen their ability to focus and refocus.

STEPS TO BRAIN CHECK

1. Focus on what you are doing using your Brain

2. Focus on what you are doing using your Eyes

3. Focus on what you are doing using your Ears

 Step 1—Focus on what you are doing using your Brain.

In her book *The Mindful Child*, Susan K. Greenland says, "Where and how children choose to direct their attention makes a huge difference in who they are and who they will become."[5] The easiest way to help your child do this is to first help him simply be aware of where his brain is focusing right now. Then ask him to make a choice about where to put his attention. You can tell your child to ask himself these questions: Where is my attention right now? Where is the best place to be putting my attention right now? Can I make the choice to shift my attention?

Once children practice this, it really will become second nature. Sophie is one of my eleven-year-old martial arts students. I was explaining an exercise to her class and all the children were sitting down facing me. When my eyes looked over in her direction, she immediately said out loud, "Oh, I just did a Brain Check and realized I wasn't paying attention." It was a moment of true self-regulation. She realized on her own that her focus wasn't on my instruction.

I responded by saying that it's totally normal and understandable to lose focus sometimes because our brain jumps around so much, but that it was really great that she caught it and chose to bring her attention back to what we were doing.

We have seen how the Body and Breath affect the Brain, but the reverse is also quite true. Top athletes are incredible examples of how the brain affects the body. Mental concentration and focus is most often what separates a good athlete from a great one. Olympic gold medalist Bruce Jenner said, "I always felt that my greatest asset was not my physical ability, it was my mental ability."

Step 2—Focus on what you are doing using your Eyes.

My six-year-old nephew absolutely loves playing Little League baseball, and whenever I am in town visiting him, he asks me to come to his games. Seeing a group of five- and six-year-olds with their miniature uniforms and mitts is always quite adorable. It's interesting how often I hear the coaches yell out, "Keep your eyes on the ball!" This isn't always directed at the batter; it's often directed toward the outfielders, who might be looking over at another game, pulling at something in the grass, spinning their baseball hat, etc., etc. These baseball games with young children are a great example of what a huge role our eyes play in our focus and attention. It's funny: sometimes the baseball scores end up looking more like basketball scores with final scores in the high double digits! This is so often because the outfielders' eyes are simply turned away and the ball rolls right by them, allowing the runners to score easily.

Whether it's playing sports, paying attention in the classroom, or focusing on homework, it's very helpful for your child to really learn to focus her eyes on the task at hand. You can remind your child that checking her eyes is a big part of helping her to focus her brain.

When I speak during school assemblies, I try to show the children how important it is to use their eyes to help with focus. I am usually standing at the front of the library or cafeteria. I'll ask all the children to look away from me, and I point to a direction where they should look. I continue talking while their eyes are all looking away. I then ask them to shift the focus of their eyes back to me and I talk once again. I then ask the students whether it was easier for them to pay attention to me when they were looking at me or not looking at me. It's always very obvious to them that they were much more focused when looking directly at me.

You can do this same exercise at home. You can also help your child to develop eye awareness by asking him to look around the room and count how many things he sees in the color red, green, orange, etc., or that have the shape of a circle, triangle, square, etc. Another fun game we like to play at summer camp is to have the children look at something or someone. Then they close their eyes and we change one thing about what they were looking at. Then we tell the children to open their eyes to see whether they can figure out the difference. Of course, you can vary these exercises in their complexity depending on the age of the child. One of the simplest ways to practice eye focus every day is to make sure you and your child maintain eye contact while talking and listening to each other.

Step 3—Focus on what you are doing using your Ears.

Just as important as checking the eyes is checking the ears. So your child will need to really practice the art of listening and self-regulate how she is using her ears to focus. I often tell children that listening is one of the hardest things to do, and I really mean it. I don't think it's an easy task for children to listen to their teachers all day. However, having them check on their ears during a Brain Check definitely gives them a concrete reminder to refocus their ears on the task at hand.

I have a few fun exercises to help children develop their listening skills. One game I like to play is called Elephant Ears. I ask the children to close their eyes. Then I ask them to raise one finger anytime they hear a different sound. It could be the air-conditioning clicking on, a lawn mower outside, a voice in another room, or different sounds that I purposefully make. This game helps them to develop their general awareness skills. Then to help them hone their focused awareness skills, I ask them to continue with their eyes closed and to pay attention only to my voice. I then vary the volume and speed of my voice and ask them to raise one finger each time they hear something different.

You can easily play this at home. For example, before reading your child a book, you can ask him to close his eyes and tell you about each different sound he can hear in the house. Then start reading and ask him to pay attention only to your voice and the different sounds, volume, and tones you make.

Of course, each child is different, and focus comes easily for some and not so easily for others. But by giving your child three easy steps to check (Brain, Eyes, and Ears), she will have a map to follow, a direct pathway for how to focus. Asking a child to do a Brain Check is so much more empowering and so much more effective than simply asking her to pay attention.

PARENTING PILLARS

To help you integrate the River Check-in with your child, let's filter the tool through the Four Parenting Pillars—Modeling; Unconditional Love and Acceptance; Nurturing and Empowering Encouragement; and Empowering Discipline.

You'll see throughout the book that we always start with **Modeling**, which really means we are always starting with you. As the parent, you are by far your child's greatest and most influential teacher. While it's extremely helpful for you to model the principles of a River Check-in and the qualities of focus and mindfulness, it's most important that you are modeling the process of this tool rather than trying to be the perfect role model. No one is perfect, and it's much better for your child to see you working with the tool rather than pretending you have it all together. So let your child see you use your *Ninja Breathing* in a traffic jam or see you do a complete Body, Breath, and Brain Check before working on your taxes. And don't be surprised when your child reminds you about your 3 Bs when you forget!

One semester I had a particularly unfocused group of students in my martial arts class at a local elementary school. It was a brand-new group of students with a wide variety of ages and focus skills in a noisy environment—not a good combination for a strong, focused class. I often found myself repeating instructions over and over and spending much of the class time just trying to rein in their attention. Did I always practice **Unconditional Love and Acceptance?** No, and I have to admit that it was difficult at times. I am telling you this story because I know that as a parent it can be frustrating when your child is not paying attention to you or when you have to repeat yourself over and over again.

When I find myself in frustrating situations like that one class, I try to remind myself that it is asking a lot of a child to always be present and mindful in today's world of fast-paced technology and excess stimuli. A child's brain is so often overstimulated, and every child has a different set point for focus and attention. As best you can, understand that each child is unique, and love and accept your child for who she is, not for what she did or didn't do. This doesn't mean you can't address her lack of focus and attention, but just be careful not to withdraw your love as a result of her behavior. This might take some practice on your part, but in the end it will be less exhausting for you. I know from many years of experience with thousands of children that when I can simply accept and respect who each child is as an individual person, I am much less engaged in any kind of power struggle. When I am not trying to control them or put up a fight to get their total focus and attention, they are more inclined to feel my love and acceptance and are much more likely to respond to my encouragement and support.

Because focus can be such a challenge for some children, your **Nurturing and Empowering Encouragement** toward them can be a great source of inspiration and strength. Remember the basic steps: Encourage your child to be *his* personal best instead of comparing himself to others; support your child in learning from mistakes or from those times when he has lost focus; and encourage your child to take responsibility for being present and mindful without constant reminders from you.

I find myself often telling my students, "I am here to remind you to do your River Check-ins, but little by little you will be able to remind yourself and then it will just become part of you." This kind of statement is very supportive, yet it's also empowering because I am letting them know I have confidence that they can take care of themselves, and I'm encouraging them to do so. Try something similar with your child. Remember to give them Roots and Wings!

If your child is having focus or attention issues at home or in school, the best way for her to improve is through her own self-regulation and through **Empowering Discipline** from you, not through some kind of reward or punishment system. Your child's own intrinsic motivation to check her 3 Bs will not only give her a stronger sense of self but will also feed her impulse to be her personal best and continue on the path of focus and mindfulness. In contrast, the behavior modification approach may get temporary results in your child's attention, but it is disempowering and won't have the same long-lasting positive results.

The best role you can play is to help your child with awareness and reflection. In other words, you can empower your child to see why he isn't focusing or paying attention and then help him to recognize how being present and mindful will be beneficial. When a student is daydreaming in my class, I might say something like, "Can you please do a quick River Check-in to notice where your attention is right now? If you find yourself daydreaming, it is common and not a bad thing, but being able to develop strong focus muscles is very important. Having strong focus muscles will help you to feel better about yourself and be your best." Do you see how Empowering Discipline can be a positive experience? It is not a negative statement, nor is it condemning or shaming the child. It's helping the child to help himself.

RIVER CHECK-IN SUMMARY

TOOL #1: RIVER CHECK-IN—3 Bs

For focus and mindfulness

BODY	BREATH	BRAIN
BODY CHECK	BREATH CHECK	BRAIN CHECK
1. Spine—long and strong 2. Muscles—not too tight, not too loose, but in the middle like a river	1. Ninja Breathing—To calm and de-stress • Slow, deep breaths in the nose and out the MOUTH 2. Fire Breathing—To energize and focus • Fast, short breaths in the nose and out the NOSE 3. River Breathing—To focus and feel good • Slow, deep breaths in the nose and out the NOSE	1. Focus on what you are doing using your: • Brain • Eyes • Ears

CHAPTER 4

TOOL #2: RIVER EFFORT FOR CONFIDENCE AND A STRONG SENSE OF SELF

The most beautiful sight in the world is a little child going confidently down the road of life after you have shown him the way.

—*Proverb*

The father of one of my students once told me that four of his close friends were each sending a child off to college. Having elementary-age children, he surveyed his friends to see what they wished they would have done differently in raising their children. Three of the four fathers said they wished they had helped their child develop more confidence.

Unfortunately, too many children are basing their confidence and self-worth on the attention they get from the outside—from the important people in their lives, from comparing themselves to others, etc. In today's world of point cards, smiley-face stickers, and candy rewards, children are learning to feel confident only when someone else rewards them for their accomplishments. If a child feels confident only when she is rewarded or when she wins or when she does better than someone else, she is basing her entire self-worth on outward circumstances. As I have seen in my own life in following the American Happiness Formula, this kind of confidence is conditional and temporary.

True and lasting confidence comes from within—from your quality of effort and from being the best *you* can be. A strong, positive sense of self emerges when you feel good about yourself and who you are. This sense of self shouldn't depend on what other people think of you.

Several times a year, we hold tournaments at my Life Ki-do Martial Arts Academy. Many traditional sports tournaments emphasize competition and winning, leaving the winners feeling elated and the others most often feeling sad, jealous, or disappointed because they thought they weren't good enough. Our tournaments, on the other hand, ask the children to focus on their River Effort, which means putting their heart into what they are doing and giving it their all. At the end of the tournament, all the children line up and we begin by asking the children to self-reflect. We ask them to close their eyes and think about whether they feel that they did their best during the tournament. If so, we tell them to imagine an invisible medal they create for themselves, and then we ask them to place that invisible medal over their head. We explain that this is the most important medal because it comes from within, can't be taken away, and can't be lost. Then before we award the physical gold, silver, and bronze medals, we tell the students that it's normal to feel good if they receive a medal and to feel sad if they don't. But we remind them that it's most important to bring their focus back to their own effort to see whether they think they did their best.

After one particular tournament, I received a very sweet thank-you e-mail from a mother whose child was known to be extremely competitive and who had won medals at the previous two tournaments. At this third tournament her son did not receive a medal, and she was very concerned that he was going to be devastated. However, when they got in the car to go home, her son told her that he'd had a great time and that he felt really good because he knew that he had put his River Effort into everything he had done. She was amazed and thrilled. That kind of intrinsic confidence is exactly what we hope for with Life Ki-do training and what any parent would hope for her child, especially when the child is leaving the nest and going off to college.

YOUR ROLE IN DEVELOPING YOUR CHILD'S CONFIDENCE

Most parents believe that praising their child with blanket statements like "You are so smart" or "You are so talented" will boost their child's confidence. It sure seems like a child could only benefit from hearing this from his mom or dad. But in fact, this kind of praise that is based on a fixed characteristic rather than effort can actually be quite detrimental. As we have seen, anxiety is often caused by the thought that one is not in control. When a child is praised for a fixed characteristic, skill, or talent, it seems unchangeable to him. However, his effort is something he can control and monitor. It is not fixed and so it leaves plenty of room for him to improve.

For many years psychologist Carol Dweck studied the effect of praise on students in a dozen New York City schools. Her research assistants tested fifth graders with puzzles easy enough that all the children would do well. Afterward, the students were randomly given praise, either for their intelligence ("You must be smart at this") or for their effort ("You must have worked really hard"). Then the students were given a choice for the second round of tests. They could choose either a test more difficult than the first, which they were told they would learn a lot from, or they could take an easy test like the first one. Of the children who were praised for their effort, an astonishing 90 percent chose the more difficult puzzles. On the other hand, the majority of those praised for their intelligence chose the easier test. Then the researchers gave all the children a much more difficult test, and predictably they all failed. But those originally praised for their effort on the first test simply assumed they hadn't focused hard enough on this third test, and they were willing to try every solution possible, with some even remarking that this was their favorite test. But those children who were originally praised for being smart assumed their failure was evidence they weren't really smart at all. These children were visibly sweating and stressed. Finally, all the children were given one last round of tests as easy as the first. Those originally praised for effort improved their original score by about 30 percent, while those originally praised for their smarts did worse by about 20 percent.[1]

It's clear that when children are praised for being smart or for some other fixed characteristic, their confidence is based so much on what you think and say that they are afraid to make a mistake or take a risk and have a hard time admitting errors. Maintaining their image becomes of primary importance, and they are more competitive and more interested in beating others. However, if children are praised for their effort, they see themselves in control of their own success. They don't tend to dwell on their mistakes, and they know that with effort they can continue to improve.

One day my ten-year-old nephew showed me his report card. He had received straight As! I was a very proud uncle, and while it would have been easiest just to give him a high five and tell him how smart he was, I told him how great his report card was, and then I asked him whether he had to put in a lot of effort to get such good grades. I was purposefully asking him to self-reflect, to take ownership for his effort. He answered that he had indeed put in much effort, and I could tell he was proud that this had paid off. His seeing the value of his effort was much more important—and will have much longer lasting results—than my praise alone.

So your role in developing your child's confidence is very much about helping her to focus on her effort. River Effort is an invaluable tool that empowers your child to develop confidence and a strong sense of self that comes from within, rather than looking to others for how she should feel about herself.

RIVER EFFORT—ICE, PUDDLE, RIVER

We tell children that River Effort helps them to feel and be their personal best. This Tool for Life gives children a tangible inner gauge to become aware of and identify their quality of effort and then to self-regulate, if necessary. The tool uses the analogies of Ice, Puddle, and River, three different qualities of effort that children can easily visualize and relate to. Ice Effort represents a state of stress and trying too hard. Puddle Effort is on the other end of the spectrum and represents a state of laziness and trying too little. River Effort is in the middle and represents a state of both strength and fluidity—putting your heart into what you are doing and giving it your all.

Once you introduce these concepts to your child, you will be amazed at how quickly he will understand the principles and start applying the language. I often hear my students talk about being too Icy or how they felt like a Puddle but most of all how good it feels when they are being like a River.

ICE EFFORT

- Trying too much

- Feeling stuck, pressured, or stressed

The analogy of Ice is easy for children to understand and relate to. Even children as young as four can immediately grasp the concept that being like Ice means trying too much or feeling stuck, pressured, or stressed. Giving children something they can easily visualize helps them to identify what they are feeling and provides them a vocabulary to talk about it.

Sometimes I like to break down the concept of Ice in relation to the three Bs. In the Body, being like Ice feels overly tight or stiff, or feeling fidgety or hyper. The Breath is usually hard, fast, short, and shallow or is being held. In the Brain, Ice manifests as pressure or anxiety or feeling stuck, nervous, overly hyper, or silly.

Usually Ice Effort is motivated by the idea that confidence and fulfillment comes from how others see you and what kinds of recognition and approval you receive from others. It often stems from the fear of not being good enough, not being as good as someone else, letting someone down, being rejected, or failure. The thought behind it may be something like, "If I try really, really hard, I will be liked or will get approval from my teacher/parent/friends." In this case, the child is extrinsically motivated and overly focused on getting rewards and avoiding punishments. Regardless of the results, Ice Effort will usually make the process or experience of the activity full of tension and pressure, which is far from fulfilling.

Even if the results of Ice Effort are successful, it's often difficult to enjoy those results because one starts feeling immediate pressure to get the next fix of success or approval. When I was in tenth grade I made the varsity wrestling team, which was not the norm for a young sophomore. My *modus operandi* was to win, win, win, and I was definitely operating from a place of Ice Effort and a fear of losing. So much so that after I won the state wrestling championship that year, I decided to quit the team. I tried to convince myself and others that I was quitting because it was unhealthy for me to lose weight in order to wrestle in my weight class. But the honest truth is that while I did get an immediate confidence high from the championship win, my confidence quickly waned because it was based predominantly on outward recognition. All I could feel was the pressure to repeat that high level of performance. It seemed better just to quit rather than fail to receive that same kind of recognition again.

My wrestling dilemma is not an uncommon one for anyone who fixates on external achievements and what others think rather than doing one's best and enjoying the process. As Mother Teresa once said, "It's not how much we do, but how much love we put into what we do."

On the other hand, if the outcome of Ice Effort is *not* successful then it's easy to feel frustrated, defensive, and dejected. In a state of Ice Effort there is so much tension and pressure that anything can trigger emotional upset. For example, two teenagers were sparring in my class one day, and one of the boys was being very Icy by focusing solely on trying to beat his opponent with brute force. When his Ice Effort didn't succeed, he became defensive, started making excuses, and then tried to blame the other student. I could see that he was going to walk away feeling very disheartened, so I took him aside to help him reflect upon his quality of effort. He realized that his whole system was inundated with Ice and that he was much too focused on the outward results and what other people were going to think of him. Instead of leaving with a broken spirit, he took the opportunity to spar in another round using less Ice, and he walked away feeling much more confident.

To help your child learn about Ice Effort, I suggest telling her that you would like her to become an Ice Detective for a moment. Explain that people often use Ice Effort when they are feeling a lot of pressure or stress to be good at something. To make it less conceptual, you can tell her a story from your own life when you used Ice Effort, or you can tell a very short story that you know she can relate to. For example, I sometimes like to tell a story about a boy named Tommy Tension who had an older sister who got a lot of praise from their parents for getting straight As. Tommy Tension felt enormous pressure to be as smart as his sister, and his focus was not on being his own personal best but rather on trying to keep up with her. He tried so hard to get good grades that poor Tommy Tension often got headaches in school from all the pressure. Turns out that Ice Effort actually made it harder for Tommy Tension to get good grades because he couldn't just focus on being his best.

After telling your child a story such as this to help her relate to the concept of Ice Effort, you can then ask whether she can think of other reasons why somebody would feel pressure to use Ice Effort. Typical answers I get from my students are wanting to beat someone else, wanting to win the prize or reward, wanting to be liked by others, or not wanting to look stupid. In my martial arts classes I often ask students to do the same drill in three different ways, using Ice, Puddle, and River Effort, to give them an experiential understanding. I was quite surprised one day when several students commented that when they were doing the drill with Ice Effort they felt like they wanted to cheat. When I asked why they said that it was because they felt pressure to beat the other students and be the best no matter what it took.

Finally, ask your child whether she can think of times or areas in her own life when she has used Ice Effort. Ask her to think about the results she achieved through Ice Effort and why she was possibly using Ice Effort to get those results. This kind of detective work builds great self-awareness. Being aware of and being able to identify and label when she is in a state of Ice is a great first step for your child to return to a state of emotional balance.

PUDDLE EFFORT

• Trying too little

• Feeling dull, lazy, or bored

The opposite of being like Ice is being like a Puddle. Continuing with the analogy of water, it's easy for children to imagine a stagnant Puddle, especially in contrast to a solid block of Ice. We explain that being like a Puddle is trying too little and feeling dull, lazy, or bored.

Breaking it down into the 3 Bs, a Body that is like a Puddle is one that is overly loose, lacking form and structure, hunched over, and often slow. The Breath is shallow and dull, and the Brain is lazy, disinterested, bored, disconnected, or apathetic.

Puddle Effort, just like Ice Effort, is extrinsically motivated. It comes from the belief that confidence is based on how others see you rather than how you feel about yourself. A common fear behind the Puddle is often that your best won't be good enough and could result in failure, which would be worse than trying very little or not trying at all. Another fear is that if you try and succeed, others will always expect the same from you. Not wanting to live with that pressure, you may think it's easier to be a Puddle and not give it your all. My decision not to continue wrestling after winning the state championship is a perfect example of some of the thoughts behind Puddle Effort—"If I don't try, then I can't fail" or "I don't want to try because I'm afraid I won't be good enough."

Puddle Effort can also be motivated by a lack of interest in the task at hand. Someone acting like a Puddle might have thoughts like the following: "This is really boring so I don't want to listen," "I don't like this so why should I even try," or the classic "There's nothing for me to do and I'm so bored."

As we all know, there are always going to be times in our lives, whether we are three years old or ninety-three years old, that we have to do things that we don't necessarily want to do. For a three-year-old this may be putting toys away or taking a bath, for a teenager it may be doing homework or adhering to a curfew, and for an adult it may be cooking dinner or mowing the lawn. The way we approach these types of activities has a large impact on our overall level of happiness and fulfillment. I often tell children that a great Ninja Secret is that in order to feel confident and happy, *how* you are doing what you are doing is more important than *what* you are doing. Using Puddle Effort can make a fun, enjoyable activity boring and uninteresting and make a mundane or nonpleasurable experience even more excruciating.

Continue with the detective theme to help your child learn about Puddle Effort. Ask him to become a Puddle Detective. Start by explaining that sometimes we feel like a Puddle when we would rather be doing something else, when we can't find something fun

or interesting to do, or when we don't feel like we will be successful with an activity so there's no use in trying. Then to help your
child further understand the concept, tell him about a time when
you have used Puddle Effort in your life. Or you can use a short
story that I like to tell: Bored Billy had lots of friends, lots of toys,
and lots of after-school activities, but he was always bored, bored,
bored. He thought his whole life was boring, but really he had a
habit of using Puddle Effort everywhere he went. He was always
slow and lazy, and he never tried at anything. Poor Bored Billy—if
only he could see that his Puddle Effort was making his life one
big bore.

After telling the story, ask your child whether he can think of
any other reason why someone might use Puddle Effort. You might
be surprised at the insightful answers you'll receive. Then to invite
self-reflection, ask your child to put on his Puddle Detective hat
and think of times or areas in his own life when he has used Puddle
Effort and why he may have felt like a Puddle. You and your child
can discuss how a lack of effort and being like a Puddle can easily
cause boredom and weaken confidence.

When Lexi first started in my martial arts classes as a kindergart-
ner, she epitomized Puddle Effort. Literally every class she came to
me with a story that exemplified her being bored, lazy, or disinterested. Her stomach hurt, her head hurt, or simply her toe hurt. She
forgot her karate pants. She needed to get a drink of water. She
needed to go to the bathroom. She didn't understand what we were

doing. She didn't like her wrestling partner. And on and on and on. But then something changed. We had been practicing Ice, Puddle, and River Effort quite a bit in class, and it all started to sink in. Without me having to directly intervene, Lexi realized all by her little five-year-old self that she was one big Puddle. After that I saw her put in more and more effort into each class. The excuses became fewer and fewer, and by the time she was in first grade she had become one of the most focused and engaged members of class. Her level of confidence had soared from a sad, apathetic little girl to a radiant and proud class leader.

RIVER EFFORT

- Putting your heart into what you are doing and giving it your all
- Feeling happy, confident, and fulfilled

In contrast to solid Ice or a stagnant Puddle, a River is strong yet fluid. A River gives children the perfect analogy for a state that represents emotional strength and balance. Rivers are always flowing and moving around obstacles; they don't get stuck. Most children understand that Rivers are also always moving toward something greater, which can inspire them to be their personal best.

Being like a River means being fluid, present and engaged—the perfect balance between tension and relaxation. In relation to the 3 Bs, the Body is relaxed yet strong, flexible, and fluid; the Breath is even, deep, purposeful, and appropriate for the activity; and the Brain is engaged, present, and receptive.

While Ice Effort and Puddle Effort are extrinsically motivated, River Effort is intrinsically motivated. It is a natural expression of one's inner strength that comes from a deep sense of self-worth. It is motivated by one's own internal fulfillment and satisfaction rather than by external recognition, such as the approval or disapproval that comes from someone else. River Effort is putting your heart into what you are doing. It is a state of full engagement and giving it your all.

The result of River Effort doesn't necessarily mean you'll win or be the best in comparison to others, but it will be the most enjoyable and fulfilling process for you, and the results will represent your personal best. This will feel good and build confidence from the inside out. I often tell children, "It is much more important that you do *your* best, rather than trying to be *the* best."

When children use River Effort, they are less likely to give up, more likely to retain information they learn, more likely to learn from their mistakes, and more likely to return to the activity again than those using Ice or Puddle Effort. Remember the studies of the children with the puzzles? Those who were praised on effort, and who thus focused more on doing their best rather than on the results, were much more likely to try a more difficult puzzle later on.

Once again, ask your child to become a detective to help her learn about being a River. If you'd like, you can use the Goldilocks story to illustrate the concept of the River. You can point out that Goldilocks was always able to find the middle way—not too hot, not too cold, but just right; not too hard, not too soft, but just right. It's the same with Effort. It's best not to try too hard like Ice or too little like a Puddle, but to be in the middle like a River by putting your heart into what you are doing and giving it your all.

Feel free to add a story from your own life about how River Effort helped you to feel confident and happy. Then for self-awareness, ask your child if he can think of times or places in his life when he has used River Effort. Discuss how it made him feel. It's great for you to acknowledge here that using River Effort will help him to develop a strong, deep inner confidence and self-respect. You can remind your child that it's not about being perfect or being the best or trying to prove something to someone else. It's about relaxing and knowing that you are enough but at the same time always feeling challenged to keep learning and growing.

HOW TO TURN FROM ICE OR PUDDLE INTO A RIVER

Being aware of and being able to identify a state of imbalance such as Ice or Puddle are great first steps to returning to the optimal state of a River. But how else can we help our children to be more like a River?

First, I like to explain to children that being Ice and Puddle are a normal part of life and are not bad. It's crucial that children understand that all of us at times experience Ice and Puddle, and these two states can help remind us when we are not flowing like a River.

In the next chapter you'll learn more about the A–B Formula, but the basics are "A" for Accept and "B" for Baby Step. Children can apply this tool to accept that they are being like Ice or a Puddle, and then they can work on one Baby Step to help them go in the direction of being like a River.

The Breath is a tangible way to both Accept and Baby Step to being more like a River. For example, I tell children that *Ninja Breathing* can melt Ice. The slow, purposeful breaths in the nose and out the mouth will help to calm and de-stress when the child is feeling like Ice. On the other hand, *Fire Breathing* can energize when the child is feeling like a Puddle. The fast breaths in and out the nose will bring energy to the lazy Puddle. Once the child feels more like a River, she can focus on the deep, even *River Breathing* in and out the nose.

The week after I taught River Effort to a second-grade class, a young girl named Scarlett raised her hand. She wanted to tell me that she had had a dance recital that week. She said when her mom was driving her there she started feeling very nervous and Icy. She said she realized she was feeling like Ice and then remembered to do her *Ninja Breathing*. She was very happy to report that it really helped her to relax, and she was able to enjoy and do her best at her dance recital. I could tell that it was a very empowering moment for her.

This little seven-year-old was able to manage and take care of her emotions in a positive way.

Another technique I like to teach children uses the Body and is one that we practice in Systema, the Russian martial art. It involves squeezing and relaxing muscles. If your child is feeling like Ice, you can ask him to breathe in, squeeze all his muscles, hold for a moment, and then release the muscles with a big, deep exhale out the mouth. This will often relieve pressure, tension, or anger. If the child is feeling like a Puddle, have her energize with short, quick squeezes and breaths, squeezing her muscles on the inhale and releasing on the exhale. This can be repeated several times to increase blood flow throughout the body and to the brain.

Of course, it's always important to remind children that another option to help them return to a River is to speak with you, a teacher, or a friend. Having the vocabulary of Ice, Puddle, and River to identify their feelings and their emotional state can make it easier for a child to reach out for help. Knowing that these feelings are normal and not bad will also help them to not judge themselves, which will make it easier for them to return to the flow of a River.

PARENTING PILLARS

All four Life Ki-do Parenting Pillars—Modeling, Unconditional Love and Acceptance, Nurturing and Empowering Encouragement, and Empowering Discipline—can help you to help your child develop his River Effort.

Of course, **Modeling** River Effort is one of the best ways to teach your child. We already talked about you discussing with your child times when you have felt Ice, Puddle, and River Effort. It's critical for children to see that while being like a River is the optimal state, Ice and Puddle are also normal and not to be feared. As long as you don't dwell on extreme cases of Ice or Puddle, it's important for your child to see you being at times off balance and then returning to being like a River. While on a family ski trip, the mom of one of my students was at the top of the slope and was starting to feel very nervous and scared. She remembered hearing about River Effort in her son's classes, so she decided to take the opportunity to talk to her son about it right then and there on top of the ski slope. She told her son that she was feeling like Ice and was scared to ski down the hill, but that she remembered hearing about *Ninja Breathing* and how it could help her to melt the Ice she was feeling inside. She later told one of our instructors that she realized how much more beneficial it was for her to model the process of doing her best and River Effort rather than pretending to her son that she had it all together. Your child will benefit greatly from seeing you approach life with this kind of attitude, and there's no doubt that your own experience of life will be more fulfilled and content.

Giving your child **Unconditional Love and Acceptance** will support and encourage her to practice River Effort. On the other hand, if you dole out love to your child based on her behavior, you are likely endorsing Ice or Puddle Effort. If you love and accept your child only when she is following the rules or being "good," she may become like Ice, constantly trying to please you and earn your love, or she may become like a Puddle, not wanting to try at all for fear of failure and fear of losing your approval. In either case, through your love and support you are unconsciously asking your child to be extrinsically motivated, and this will not build a strong, inner confidence. If, however, you love and accept your child for who she is and not for what she does or doesn't do, you are helping to strengthen her confidence and intrinsic motivation to do her best and be like a River.

Another great way to inspire your child to be his personal best is through **Nurturing and Empowering Encouragement**. One of the steps in this Parenting Pillar is to encourage your child to be his best instead of comparing himself to others. I know that there is enormous peer pressure and media influence on today's modern child to live up to a certain unrealistic ideal. You might find that your child easily falls into this trap. But you can really help your child to step out of this endless struggle by offering Nurturing and Empowering Encouragement—supporting your child in learning from his mistakes and encouraging him to be *his* best, not *the* best.

Empowering Discipline is a wonderful approach to help your child reflect on and resolve her own problems when she is being either like Ice or Puddle. Instead of swiftly issuing a punishment or shaming your child if she has misbehaved or made a mistake, this approach will empower your child to learn how to self-regulate for the next time. This technique may take more time initially, but it will definitely have longer-reaching results.

The first step is to enter into a conversation with your child with a team approach mind-set, respecting what your child has to say and inviting her to self-reflect, rather than you immediately labeling and trying to correct her behavior. Using the vocabulary of Ice, Puddle, and River should be very helpful for your child to identify and become aware of her motivation and effort in any situation. Then it's helpful if you can assist your child in learning not to judge herself but to see that mistakes and challenges are opportunities for growth and improvement. In my classes, I often have to address a child who may be acting out and not participating with the group. Instead of shaming or blaming, I try to invite that child to see why she is acting out and being like Ice, or not participating and being like a Puddle. I remind my students that the kind of attention they will get from being like Ice or Puddle will not be nearly as good as the feeling they will get from being their best and doing their River Effort.

RIVER EFFORT SUMMARY

TOOL #2: RIVER EFFORT—ICE, PUDDLE, RIVER

For confidence and a strong sense of self

ICE	PUDDLE	RIVER
1. Trying too much 2. Feeling stuck, pressured, or stressed	1. Trying too little 2. Feeling dull, lazy, or bored	1. Putting your heart into what you are doing and giving it your all 2. Feeling happy, confident, and fulfilled

TOOL #3: A–B FORMULA FOR RESILIENCE AND THE ABILITY TO DEAL WITH LIFE'S CHALLENGES

More than education, more than experience, more than training, a person's level of resilience will determine who succeeds and who fails. That's true in the cancer ward, it's true in the Olympics, and it's true in the boardroom.
—*Dean Becker,* Harvard Business Review, *May 2002*

As any mama bear or papa bear knows, our first and foremost instinct as a parent is to protect our children from harm. There's no doubt that these animal instincts are vital in the survival and nurturing of our offspring. The tricky part is that while we need to protect our children, we also need to empower them with the skills to protect and take care of themselves.

I know that it's hard to see a sad face and not want to fix everything for your child. But when you swoop in and "fix" instead of helping your child you are cheating her out of the learning experience of being unhappy—learning that the condition is not permanent and she will get through it. One of your most important roles as a parent is to prepare your child to maneuver the ups and downs of life with the critical skill of resilience, the ability to bounce back. Unfortunately, the only way for your child to really learn resilience is to actually work through times of challenge, adversity, or loss.

To help your child navigate his way through challenging times, you can arm him with the A–B Formula, a blueprint for help when he is having a hard time with what he is feeling or doing. This tool is also a tangible way for children to deal with negative and limited views or beliefs about themselves—the inner judge or scorekeeper that's inside all of our heads.

The A–B Formula is simple and easy for children to remember and use: "A" = Accept and "B" = Baby Step. These two steps, accepting where you are today and taking a step in the direction you want to go, are key elements to resilience.

True acceptance of whom and where you are today is an absolutely critical step in being able to face adversity. Acceptance is the starting point for movement and growth. If your child can accept her current state of mind or the conditions she finds herself in, then she is accepting who she is, and this is key to building self-worth. Once this baseline acceptance and self-worth is in place, she can then feel open to the possibility of being and doing more.

To move forward, a Baby Step helps ignite the momentum for change to happen. As long as the step is small enough to be achievable, it will build the confidence and motivation necessary to keep moving in a positive direction.

The A–B Formula will help your child to see change and adversity as something that can be met with incremental steps rather than something that's unfair, overwhelming, and to be avoided. With this healthy and balanced approach, he will be able to build long-term resilience, which in turn will contribute to his self-esteem and positive outlook on life.

STUDY OF RESILIENCE

The psychological study of resilience began only about forty or fifty years ago. Psychologists who were studying children growing up in high-risk environments realized that some of these youngsters developed quite well despite the poverty, violence, poor parenting, or hunger they faced. But many of these children became victims of their surroundings. It was clear that the children who thrived possessed a resilience that the others did not.

At first, many believed that the resilient youngsters had an extraordinary genetic makeup that made them invulnerable to harm. You were either born with it or not.[1] But more recent research has indicated that while some children do have a natural predisposition toward resilience, it is something that can be learned by all. So no, there's no magic pill, but the great news is that we can actually help our children develop the critical skill of resilience.

Studies have shown that children who develop resilience are not only more likely to develop faster, but they will generally be happier than children who don't have a great ability to bounce back. According to Bonnie Benard, of the University of Minnesota's National Resilience Resource Center, resilient children have more social competence, problem-solving ability, autonomy, and sense of purpose and future.

"For youth to become resilient, they must feel that they have the ability to do something about their situations—to meet their challenges. When they have doubt about their ability to find a successful solution, feelings of depression are in the making," says Edith H. Grotberg of the International Resiliency Project. So to help your child successfully meet challenges, teach her the A–B Formula and watch her inner strength bloom.

A = ACCEPT

The first step in the A–B Formula is "A" for Accept. It is the less active of the two steps and so can easily be overlooked, but it's important that children learn to accept their current state, whether that is having a hard time hitting a tennis ball over the net, learning long division, feeling jealous that an older sibling has more privileges, or dealing with sadness about being left out.

When a child accepts what he is feeling or accepts his current level of skill or ability, he is acknowledging his worth as the person he is today, giving him fertile ground to move forward. It not only teaches him to be tolerant and nonjudgmental of himself, but it actually helps him to be more tolerant and less judgmental of others as well.

If a child is not able to accept her current state, it often makes the thought, feeling, or emotion much stronger. If this becomes a regular pattern, then those feelings get pushed down and buried so deep inside that a child's unconscious belief about herself becomes something like, "I'm not good enough or lovable enough," "Something is wrong with me," or "If they only knew." Nathaniel Branden, a psychologist who is a pioneer in the field of self-esteem and personal development, says, "I cannot be truly myself, cannot build self-esteem, if I cannot accept myself."[2]

Psychologist Martin Seligman says that feeling bad can actually help us learn to become more optimistic and to overcome feelings of helplessness. So you might explain to your child that while certain feelings and emotions might not feel very good, moving through them will actually help him to be stronger and happier. However, helping your child to see a difficult situation or feeling as an opportunity for growth is not always easy and requires timing and tact on your part. When your child is in a heightened emotional state, he is being ruled by his limbic system, the emotional, nonrational part of the brain. This is not the time to talk about lessons that can be learned. Your child won't be able to take in what you are saying, and he can feel hurt and judged, which can shut him down or make him want to shut you down. This is the classic scene of a child running to his room, slamming the door, and yelling, "You don't understand!"

So the key ingredient is to give your child plenty of Unconditional Love and Acceptance, and then add a dash of compassion. If she feels your empathy, understanding, and support and is given time to return to the more rational part of her brain, she will be much more receptive to learning or growing from the situation.

A young boy named Charlie was playing a computer video game. The program crashed, he lost all his points, and then he lost his marbles. While a meltdown over a video game can seem to be trivial, it's still an incredible learning opportunity. Instead of completely dismissing Charlie's feelings as unreasonable, his wise grandmother empathized with him and likened his situation to when her computer crashed and she lost a report she had been working on. Charlie felt understood instead of shut down, which most likely would have happened if his grandmother had told him he was overreacting and then threatened to take the video game away if he didn't stop his whining by the count of three.

In this situation, it was crucial that Charlie accepted his feelings of frustration, because as Grandma knows, he can expect to have this feeling many times in his life. If he can learn as a child to accept the frustration, he'll be much better equipped to deal with it later on when it comes up again. Accepting the frustration also gives him the best chance of processing the emotion quickly and taking a step to help himself out of the situation.

"Dr. Happiness" himself, psychologist Richard Diener, is very clear that while most pop psychology emphasizes positive thinking and affirmations, experiencing our negative emotions and accepting them will actually have a significant impact on our lasting happiness.

STEPS TO ACCEPT

Now that you know the importance of the Accept part of the A-B Formula, let me show you how to break that down for your child into three easy steps:

1. Be aware of where you are today

2. Be kind and patient with yourself

3. Take responsibility instead of blaming others

. . .

Step 1 — Be Aware of Where You Are Today

This first step starts with awareness. Your child might need your help to become aware of and identify what she is feeling. But the point is to empower your child with the skill of self-awareness. So before jumping in to give your opinion, first see whether your child can identify her own feelings. If she is not able to do this, then you can help her by asking questions, or you can give her a few options and ask her to pick the one that most closely matches how she is feeling.

For example, if your child walks in from school noticeably upset, you might say, "You look upset. Can you tell me what you are feeling?" If the child can't explain, you might say, "Are you feeling sad? Did someone say or do something at school that hurt your feelings? Are you afraid to tell me something that you did at school?" Asking your child to take a snapshot of what's happening right now will allow him to acknowledge those feelings, and this is the first critical step to acceptance.

A ten-year-old student shared with me that she had dyslexia. She said that in the past taking tests was particularly difficult for her even though she was given a little extra time. But after learning the awareness part of acceptance, she was able to identify that the pressure she felt about being dyslexic was creating high levels of anxiety about tests. She was ecstatic to tell me about her discovery that her anxiety was actually causing more problems for her than her learning disability. Of course, tests still posed difficulties for her, but accepting her situation dramatically decreased her feelings of stress and tension, and she was therefore able to do her very best.

Step 2 — Be Kind and Patient with Yourself

In his book *The Optimistic Child*, professor Martin Seligman says, "Depressed children and adults are forever blaming themselves . . . and being a chronic self-blamer increases a child's risk for depression."[3] When children judge themselves harshly, they might think they are stuck, and it will be much harder for them to move forward because of their own self-imposed limitations. However, if a child can learn to be kind and patient with herself, it gives her room to improve and the fuel to grow.

In martial arts I learned the Japanese term *kaizen,* which means "consistent and never ending self-improvement." This rang so true for me and relieved me of the belief that I was supposed to be perfect at everything and for everyone. The pressure, stress, and self-judgment that tagged along with that belief were replaced with kindness and patience toward myself. I learned that life is a process to enjoy, not a stressed-out path of chasing never-ending goals. In her book, *Mindset: The New Psychology of Success,* Stanford professor of psychology Carol Dweck claims that people usually have one of two basic mind-sets. Those with a fixed mind-set believe talents and abilities are innate—you either have them or you don't. Those with a growth mind-set think that talents can be developed and that success is based on continual learning and effort. Dweck argues that a growth mind-set will allow a person to live a less stressful and more successful life. Unless you are able to be kind and patient with yourself, I don't believe that one can truly experience the essence of kaizen or a growth mind-set.[4]

For example, say Maddie is doing her math homework and she can't seem to remember her 9 times table. If Maddie is stuck in a fixed mind-set, she might claim that she is terrible at math, a broad self-judgment. This can make the situation seem overwhelming and hopeless, causing her to want to give up all together. She has put herself inside a box labeled "Bad at Math." This label can seem to be affixed with superglue, and thus it's hard to see a way out of the box. However, if Maddie is reminded about step 2 of Accept, Be Kind and Patient with Yourself, she may find herself in a growth mind-set and be able to focus just on the situation at hand, which is very specifically about the 9 times table. From here, it will be much easier to accept the situation and think of a Baby Step that can help her move forward.

To help your child learn to be kind to himself, you can explain that it is human nature to experience negative emotions. When children have negative emotions, they can be so overwhelmed that they actually believe they are the only ones to have those types of feelings and that something must be wrong with them. Realizing their feelings of sadness, jealousy, anger, and frustration are normal can really take the sting out and help your child look at himself with kindness rather than disdain. The problem is not experiencing the negative emotion; the problem is when he judges the emotion and beats himself up about it.

In order for children to learn patience with themselves, it's important for you to let them know that negative emotions don't last. When children encounter negative experiences they may think that they will *always* feel that way, but research shows this is not true. When I was in the hospital with my brother after he attempted to take his life, the doctor turned to me with great sadness in his heart and said, "I just wish that you kids could see that things do change."

It's so very important for your child to realize that *everyone* experiences challenges, setbacks, and stress in their lives and that these times are normal, inevitable, temporary—and great opportunities to build inner strength.

Step 3 — Take Responsibility Instead of Blaming Others

"It's his fault." "She started it." "He hit me first." We've all heard plenty of that! Blaming others happens so quickly and so often, it can seem like a reflex action. Much of the time, a child is really just trying to avoid getting into trouble, but the habit of blaming others can actually be quite detrimental.

When a child blames someone else, she is essentially giving up responsibility and the ability to make a change. Blaming can be quite disempowering. It may give the child a temporary boost of self-esteem since her lack of ability or her sad, angry or hurt feelings can be attributed to someone else, but the self-esteem boost won't last and doesn't allow the child to move forward. Blaming others is usually a means of avoidance and can delay addressing the feelings or worse yet, bury them further down.

Eleven-year-old Max was in a town basketball league. One day he came home from practice and told his dad that his coach was a loser and a terrible coach. Having attended a few practices and most games, Max's dad knew that this was not quite an accurate assessment. It was obvious Max was feeling ashamed about his abilities and he didn't know how to process those feelings, so he threw them toward the coach. Max's dad knew that his job was not only to make sure Max didn't go around calling people "loser" but also to help his son take responsibility for his feelings and work through them.

Sometimes a situation happens that is clearly not the fault of the child. Not blaming others doesn't mean accepting responsibility for something you didn't do. But it does mean always looking for your part or your responsibility in the situation.

B = BABY STEP

The second component in the A–B Formula is "B" for Baby Step. After the child has accepted his current situation, whether that is something he is feeling or something he is doing, he is ready to move forward. Taking a palatable and achievable Baby Step kick-starts the child's confidence and gives him the fuel to keep going.

Usually, focusing on a goal without having baby steps to get there can lead to stress and a feeling of being overwhelmed. If there is no clear direction or path, it's hard for the child to see through her emotions to know that she won't always be stuck. However, taking just one Baby Step helps to develop resilience and will lead the way out. The Baby Step will help the child to feel responsible for herself and capable of making a change. Starting at the age of four, children can usually make plans and complete tasks, so even very young children can understand this concept and apply it in their lives.

STEPS TO ACCEPT

In their book, *The Power of Full Engagement*, Jim Loehr and Tony Schwartz say, "Because change requires moving beyond our comfort zone, it is best initiated in small and manageable increments."[5] To help children accomplish this, I created two parts to taking a Baby Step:

1. Take a step in the direction you want to go

2. Make it a step you can handle today

. . .

Step 1 — Take a Step in the Direction You Want to Go

To build their confidence and their resilience muscles, children need to see that they are improving. Taking a step that will lead them in the direction they want to go will put them on a path to progress. This applies to emotional states as well as to mental skills, physical abilities, or interpersonal situations.

If your daughter is feeling sad because she was left out of a game on the playground and thus thinks she is not wanted or liked, you can help her accept her sad and hurt feelings and then help her find one Baby Step. Maybe it's finding a trusted friend and initiating a game between just the two of them. If your son is feeling nervous and anxious about how much he has to memorize for the lead in the school play, you can ask him to think of one Baby Step that will help him to remember his lines. Maybe it's to start by focusing on just one act, or maybe it's to find a friend in the play who he can rehearse lines with at home.

One of my students had a younger brother Ben who watched his older brother's classes from the waiting room for many years. Ben was very shy and introverted and spent much of the class time quietly engaged in drawing. Secretly, he really wished to jump into class, but he just didn't feel comfortable. He took a trial class, but he shut down and ran out. When I started an after-school class at his elementary school, Ben, his mother, and I agreed that this might be a great Baby Step that would take Ben in the direction he wanted to go. Since he was familiar and comfortable with the school environment, he agreed to join in. Taking this Baby Step allowed Ben to thrive, and after taking a year of classes at his school, he felt that he was ready to take classes at our dojo. Today you would never believe that this confident, young boy on the mats was the same shy boy who hunkered down in the waiting room.

Step 2—Make It a Step You Can Handle Today

The wise old adage "Don't bite off more than you can chew" has been around a long time for a reason. Make It a Step You Can Handle Today is exactly that. It allows children to gain mastery slowly, which will improve their feelings of self-efficacy, their belief that they can reach their goals. In order to be motivated to take a step, a child needs to know that the step is achievable. It's very important that children don't try to jump from A to Z right away.

Taking a giant or elephant step can cause anxiety, tear down confidence, and make the child feel afraid to try new things. On the flip side, taking a step that's too small usually leads to boredom and a lack of motivation to keep going. For your child to really learn the art of resilience and how to bounce back, the Baby Step should allow him to feel like a River and thus appropriately engaged and challenged.

Sometimes your child might need your help in finding the appropriate Baby Step that will take him in the direction he wants to go and that he can handle today. Always start by first asking the child if he can think of a Baby Step. If his suggestion seems too challenging and you think it may shut him down, then you might say something like, "Wow—that would be an elephant step for me. How about if we brainstorm together to see if we can break it down into smaller Baby Steps?" The point is that you are still inviting your child into the process of finding a Baby Step instead of just dismissing his idea and telling him what you think he should do.

If your child's suggestion seems dangerous or hurtful to himself or anyone else, then it's important to address that without dampening his creative impulse. Try not to immediately judge any ideas as good or bad. Instead help the child to self-evaluate his ideas so that he can learn to make good decisions on his own. Asking questions is a great way to help him to self-evaluate.

If your child can't come up with a Baby Step suggestion, you can offer some possibilities, but it's important that the child takes ownership of which Baby Steps are right for her. You might offer your suggestions as questions, asking your child if it's something she thinks will lead her in the direction she wants to go and if she thinks it is something she can handle today. It should be a team effort rather than you, as the adult, telling the child what to do. Remember that you are always trying to empower your child and inspire intrinsic motivation instead of having her think she is doing something because you told her to or because she wants to please you.

In the beginning, you might need to walk through this process step-by-step with your child, but don't be surprised when it becomes second nature for him. I have heard many stories from my students about how they used the A–B Formula on their own to process an emotion or get through a challenging time.

Nine-year-old Hayley told me that she was taking gymnastics classes after school. She said that she had wanted to give up and never go back because she just couldn't seem to master any of the skills. She was definitely feeling overwhelmed and overly challenged. She told me that after she learned the A–B Formula, she realized that the steps her gymnastics teacher had given her were too big for her to handle. She decided to take the initiative and break down the steps the teacher was giving her into smaller steps that were appropriately challenging for her. She no longer felt shut down because she had a tangible plan that she knew she could accomplish. Not only did her confidence in gymnastics improve, but she felt empowered because she was able to take care of herself and knew that she would be able to do the same in other areas of her life.

USING A–B FORMULA FOR GOAL SETTING

Since our culture places such high emphasis on competition, winning, grades, and test scores, children today are conditioned to focus more on end results than the process and enjoyment of improving and learning. Additionally, if a child does not reach her goals, which is often the case, she can feel shame, think she is a failure, and lose motivation. Achieving goals alone will never make anyone happy in the long run. But it's who you become along the way that will give you the deepest fulfillment.

Our approach to goal setting is to use the A–B Formula to create directional goals and become more process focused rather than results fixated. To make progress and improve in any area of life, the first step is to become aware of and accept where you are today. Then decide on a direction and lay out a flexible roadmap of digestible Baby Steps to take you in that direction.

PARENTING PILLARS

The four Life Ki-do Parenting Pillars—Modeling, Unconditional Love and Acceptance, Nurturing and Empowering Encouragement, and Empowering Discipline—are all key elements in helping your child develop resilience with the A–B Formula.

As with everything else, it's so important for children to see you **Modeling** resilience. Your child will learn so much from your example in how you deal with your own setbacks, mistakes, or challenges. For example, in a conversation at dinner time you can tell your children about a mistake you made at work and how you used the A–B Formula to accept that mistake and take one Baby Step to rectify the situation. Or when appropriate, you can even ask your child to help you work through the A–B Formula in a situation. It is of great benefit for a child to see failure and challenges as normal, as something that everyone faces, and as learning opportunities for growth. It makes him feel less alone and more willing to deal with his own personal challenges. Just be sure anything you share is age appropriate and not too personal or too much for your child to handle.

Sometimes when children come to my academy for the first time, they feel shy and nervous, hiding behind Mom or Dad. I usually stoop down so that I can talk to them more at their eye level. Then I often tell them about a time when I first started something new and how I felt shy and afraid too. I tell them how it's totally normal to feel that way and that sometimes you just need to take a Baby Step, like doing some *Ninja Breathing* or watching the class for a few minutes before jumping in. It's amazing to see the look on their faces. They always look so surprised that a grown-up has the same feelings as they do. It completely disarms them and helps them to accept their feelings as normal. In these cases, Modeling is extremely effective at putting a child at ease and making them feel included and part of the team.

Unconditional Love and Acceptance is a stepping-stone from which your child can learn the "A" part of the A–B Formula to accept herself. As we all know, it's not always easy to accept who we are today, but by wholeheartedly accepting your child you are mirroring the way she can be toward herself. The child will be more willing to express her true feelings and accept those feelings if she knows your love and acceptance is unwavering. It's so important for your child to know she is supported in what she is feeling and that it's okay to have those feelings, without indulging in them or getting stuck in them. Feeling Unconditional Love and Acceptance from you will give your child the foundation to feel safe, secure, and willing to challenge herself to live up to her full potential. If she doesn't trust your Unconditional Love and Acceptance, she might try to hide who she is by putting on a mask of overcompensation, avoidance, or defensiveness.

Sometimes it's hard for parents to accept their child's feelings because they can't relate to the child. A child's emotions often seem unwarranted for the situation and trivial, absurd, or overwrought to an adult. Here's where it's very helpful to practice My Shoes, Your Shoes, Our Shoes, which we'll talk more about in the next chapter. Really put yourself in your child's shoes and see what it feels like to be him. It's helpful to try to relate more to the feelings of your child rather than to his particular situation or what triggered those feelings. For example, if your daughter lost her doll and is devastated, you might not be able to relate to the magnitude of her outcry and might try to simply replace the missing doll. But if you put yourself in her shoes, you might see that you have just lost your best friend. Think about how it would feel to you if you lost your best friend, and then top that with someone telling you to stop crying, that it's no big deal, and that your friend is easily replaced. Having respect for your child and true empathy will go a long way in accepting how your child is feeling.

For the "B" part of the A–B Formula, **Nurturing and Empowering Encouragement** will help your child find the Baby Step she needs to take to move forward. This type of encouragement creates an environment that feels safe for your child to take risks in and learn from their mistakes or "weaker" areas.

Remember that to be empowering, your encouragement should inspire intrinsic motivation. This means not feeding your child all the answers even when you think you know better, you are rushed, or you want to save him from hurt or disappointment. For example, as we mentioned before, it's always best to ask your child for his own suggestions for taking a Baby Step before offering your advice. You will be nurturing his problem-solving skills, helping him to be more accountable, and helping him to feel more in control of his life. And as we know by now, research shows us that children who feel that they have more control over their own lives are generally much happier.

The fourth Parenting Pillar, **Empowering Discipline**, is another critical way for you to help your child embody the A–B Formula. The safe and trusting environment that is created by the first two steps of Empowering Discipline, a *Team Approach* and *Ground and Connect*, directly supports a child in being able to accept challenges and mistakes. Since the child won't be preoccupied with trying to get a reward or avoid a punishment, she will be in a much better position to address challenges head-on and work through them with Baby Steps. In fact, punishment will often turn her in the exact opposite direction of acceptance, because the shame and fear associated with it can either shut her down or result in her defensiveness.

The last step to Empowering Discipline, *Reflect and Resolve*, will help your child learn to take a Baby Step in the direction of making better choices. Instead of you issuing your commands for how a child should resolve a situation, asking the child to reflect on his behavior and involving the child in coming up with a solution encourages him to take responsibility for his own Baby Steps. Taking ownership of a Baby Step will give him intrinsic motivation that will have positive, long-lasting results on his behavior and well-being.

A–B FORMULA SUMMARY

TOOL #3: A-B FORMULA

For resilience and the ability to deal with life's challenges

A = ACCEPT	B = BABY STEP
1. Be aware of where you are today 2. Be kind and patient with yourself 3. Take responsibility instead of blaming others	1. Take a step in the direction you want to go 2. Make it a step you can handle today

CHAPTER 6

TOOL # 4: MY SHOES, YOUR SHOES, OUR SHOES FOR SOCIAL INTELLIGENCE

The only thing that really matters in life are your relationships to other people.
—George Vaillant, psychiatrist and professor at Harvard Medical School

One day I asked a group of my students what makes them happy. While I did get a few cute answers like hot dogs and Scooby Doo, and some expected answers like playing video games, I heard from many that it's their friends and their family that make them happy. Playdates with school friends, going fishing with their grandfather, riding bikes to the park with their family—these were all great examples of the social interactions that make a rich and happy life for a child. Not coincidentally, we find that those facing the end of their lives will most often claim that their most precious and meaningful times were those shared with friends and family.

The quality of our lives is thus quite often determined by the quality of our relationships, and everyone from seventeenth-century poets to modern-day neuroscientists knows this to be true. We've all heard the words "No man is an island." But did you know that English poet John Donne wrote those words centuries ago in 1624? His words ring so true that he is still quoted to this day, and his words have been borrowed for everything from book titles to movie titles to song lyrics. One of today's leading neuroscientists, Andrew Newberg, MD, echoes Donne's sentiment in his scientific studies of the brain. He says, "Any form of social isolation will damage important mechanisms in the brain, leading to aggression, depression, and various neuropsychiatric disorders."[1]

Yet today children are faced with various obstacles to healthy social interactions. The first major and obvious obstacle is technology. Children spend an enormous amount of time with a video game as their primary companion. All too often they are offered a cell phone with its myriad games as a form of babysitting and keeping quiet, and their abbreviated text messages have replaced verbal communication with friends.

In contrast, one of my childhood friends was reminiscing about how we grew up years ago. He remembers very clearly that on the first day of summer vacation, his mother handed him his bike and said, "Here—have a great summer!" That was it. There were no summer camps, no playdates, no organized activities, and no video games—they didn't yet exist. Yet my friend loved those long summers. Why? Because he had all summer to just ride his bike around and play with his friends, and what could be better than that! As a child, he had no idea of the value those summers gave him, but today those strong social skills he learned through play have been instrumental in helping him to become a successful business owner as well as a loving father and husband.

The second major obstacle to healthy relationships stems from social conditioning. As we have seen, most of us have been conditioned to be extrinsically motivated and to believe that our value comes from the praise and recognition of others rather than from our own personal effort and fulfillment. Thus it's easy to see other people as either an impediment to our success or as the answer to it. Neither conclusion is true, and both can lead to very unfulfilling relationships.

In fact, it's very common for us to see other people through the lens of what I call the 3 Cs—Compare, Compete, or Control. But in order to have fulfilling relationships, we must be able to connect with others on a deep emotional level. This can be accomplished through understanding, empathy, compassion, teamwork, and clear, honest communication.

So while the first three Tools for Life empower children with the focus, confidence, and resilience to develop their inner strength, the fourth tool teaches children the interpersonal and social skills they need for strong, positive, and healthy relationships. Based on mutual acknowledgment, care, and respect, My Shoes, Your Shoes, Our Shoes is a much healthier alternative to the 3 Cs—Compare, Compete, or Control.

We tell the children that My Shoes is learning to clearly and honestly express yourself because no one knows what it's like to be you. Your Shoes is learning how to hear, understand, empathize, and care about the thoughts and feelings of others. And Our Shoes is learning how to work together in a way that respects both people's thoughts and feelings. In other words, the fourth Tool for Life helps you to be a good friend to yourself, to others, and to work as a team.

THE LINK BETWEEN HEALTHY RELATIONSHIPS AND HAPPINESS

Research has shown unequivocally that having strong, meaningful relationships contributes to our overall happiness, fulfillment, and well-being. The Grant Study is the longest longitudinal study of adult life ever conducted. It has followed a group of 268 Harvard graduates for over a staggering seventy years, creating an unprecedented database of life histories. When asked what he has learned from the Grant Study, Harvard psychiatrist George Vaillant, director of the study, responded, "The only thing that really matters in life are your relationships to other people."[2] From the remarkable amount of data collected and mined, Vaillant observes, "Adolescent social class, intelligence, treadmill endurance, and constitution meant little to successful aging . . . In contrast, capacity for empathic relationships predicted a great deal."[3]

Psychologist Mark Holder and his colleagues at the University of British Columbia in Canada studied children aged eight to twelve. Their research specifically showed that those children who feel that their lives have meaning and value and who develop deep, quality relationships are happier than those who do not.[4]

As mentioned in chapter 1, an important 2002 study by Edward "Dr. Happiness" Diener and Martin Seligman, founder of Positive Psychology, found that the very happiest students from those they surveyed had rich and satisfying social relationships, spent the most time socializing, and spent the least time alone.[5]

In his 2011 book *Flourish*, Seligman adds two important elements to his long-term formula for happiness and well-being. Accomplishment is one element, and unsurprisingly, positive relationships make up the other missing element. Seligman claims that positive relationships are key to "the connected life" and that they are a basic element of well-being. He says, "Other people are the best antidote to the downs of life and the single most reliable up."[6]

Dr. Daniel J. Siegel, a neuropsychiatrist at the University of California–Los Angeles, sums up the critical importance of positive relationships. He says, "Scientific studies of longevity, medical and mental health, happiness, and even wisdom point to supportive relationships as the most robust predictor of these positive attributes in our lives across the life span."[7]

MY SHOES

Mandy was a young girl in a third-grade class in which I once worked. She was extremely bright but painfully shy. One day, I was observing a group project in which the class was engaged. Each group had to work together to plan a vacation. In a group dominated by a couple of eager boys, Mandy's voice was never heard and she just went along with their decisions. When it came time to pick restaurants for their trip, she became visibly upset to the point of tears. At this point, I stepped in and asked her if we could play My Shoes, Your Shoes, Our Shoes. I knew she needed help in expressing herself. We went through the steps and Mandy was able to clearly express herself in My Shoes, letting everyone know that she is a vegetarian and needed a restaurant with vegetarian options. Instead of shutting down, she was able to communicate her needs, and from that point on she became more engaged with the group and her confidence soared.

I always tell children that being a good friend starts with you. It's so important to be aware and sensitive to your own thoughts, feelings, and needs, and to be able to clearly communicate them. My Shoes is a critical step for children like Mandy who are like a Puddle, shy and not expressive, but it is also equally important for those who are like Ice, outspoken, brash, and opinionated. On that end of the spectrum, children tend to scream, blame, and whine. My Shoes is learning to communicate like a River—slowly, clearly, and calmly.

STEPS TO MY SHOES

To help children with their communication skills, we have broken down My Shoes into three basic steps:

1. Express clearly your thoughts and feelings
2. Explain instead of Blame
3. Speak instead of Scream

Step 1—Express Clearly Your Thoughts and Feelings

I often tell children that it's important that people know their insides, not just their outsides. I tell them that the only way others can really understand their insides and what they are thinking and feeling is if they can express themselves clearly.

It's important that children understand that My Shoes is not just about what they think they should say or what they think someone wants to hear. It's about what they are actually feeling—what's in their heart. In other words, My Shoes is about being genuine rather than just coming up with the right words to say.

An important step in clear communication is for the child to take a moment to think before she speaks so that she knows what she wants to say. When children are hurt, scared, angry, or confused, it's often difficult for them to explain their true feelings, so they blurt out sweeping generalizations such as "I don't like you," "I don't want to be your friend anymore," or "Leave me alone." It's helpful to remind your child that she should be specific when expressing her thoughts and feelings. A better choice might be, "It hurt my feelings today when you said or did _____" or "I really like having you as my friend, but it doesn't feel good to me when you _____."

Step 2—Explain Instead of Blame

"It's his fault!" "She hit me first!" Sound familiar? Blaming is very often a child's first line of defense. After teaching your child step 1, you will see how step 2 to My Shoes, Explain Instead of Blame, eventually seeps into his consciousness so that blaming someone is not always the first thing that comes out of his mouth.

It's helpful to remind your child not to focus on what the other person did; she should focus more on how she is feeling or what she is thinking about the situation. Taking responsibility for her thoughts and feelings can be very empowering. Conversely, putting all the blame on someone else doesn't give your child room to change anything that could make her feel better or improve her situation. Additionally, blaming someone else is almost guaranteed to cause the other person to become defensive and shut down open communication.

Step 3 — Speak Instead of Scream

As I'm sure you may know, some children have the tendency to use screaming as their chosen form of communication. Step 3 to My Shoes is a reminder to Speak instead of Scream, and it teaches the delivery of clear, calm communication.

You can help your child by using the analogies of Ice, Puddle, and River. If he is screaming or speaking too fast or too intensely, then you can remind him to be less like Ice and to speak more clearly and calmly like a River. You might say, "I can tell that you are really excited right now. It would be easier for me to take in what you are saying if you could speak a little softer and slower, more like a River. It helps me to do some *Ninja Breathing* when I need to slow down."

On the other hand, if your child is being very shy and is not able to communicate her needs or feelings, encourage stronger expression by gently reminding her to be less like a Puddle and to speak with the strength of a River. For example, you could say, "What you are saying is very important to me, but I'm having a hard time taking it in. Can you please speak a little louder for me so that your words are a little stronger, like a River?"

Speak instead of Scream is not about asking your child to stifle his emotions or about trying to control your child. If you use Ice, Puddle, and River as commands or reprimands, you will most likely be met with resistance and resentment. So it's helpful if you can give your child specific, tangible, and actionable suggestions about his communication, such as volume, speed, posture, eye contact, and breathing. You can use the Parenting Pillars to make sure that your words sound like an open and helpful invitation to your child.

YOUR SHOES

Your Shoes is about helping your child to develop empathy, care, and compassion. We tell children that Your Shoes is about putting yourself in the other person's shoes to try and understand what it feels like to be her. Your Shoes is forgetting yourself for a moment, listening quietly, and trying to understand the other person's thoughts, feelings, and needs and what's best for her.

Let's return to Mandy's third-grade group project. Your Shoes was an important component in helping the children learn to work together to plan their pretend vacations. Before I asked Mandy to express Her Shoes about being a vegetarian and wanting to pick a restaurant that had options for her, I explained to the two dominant boys that it would be great for them to use Your Shoes to really feel and understand what it was like to be Mandy. After she spoke up, the boys admitted that they could understand how she would feel left out if they chose a burger place that had no vegetarian options. I could tell that the boys not only listened to her words but that they had an emotional understanding of what it would feel like to be in her position. It was a critical step to finding a way for all three to work together.

STEPS TO YOUR SHOES

To help your child develop empathy, care, and compassion, the three steps to Your Shoes are:

1. Feel and understand what it's like to be in the other person's shoes

2. Listen with your ears, eyes, and heart

3. Open your mind and close your mouth

Step 1—Feel and Understand What It's Like to Be in the Other Person's Shoes

Step 1 helps children learn empathy, which is understanding and vicariously experiencing the feelings of another. Social scientists believe that empathy is central to forming healthy relationships throughout life. However, empathic listening is a skill that needs to be developed. Most often when we are listening to someone else, either we are only half listening or we are planning on what we are going to say in response. Empathic listening is about trying to see the world from someone else's perspective. You don't have to agree with the other person. You just need to try to understand that person's frame of reference. The easiest way to explain this to children is to tell them that step 1 to Your Shoes is about trying to feel and understand what it's like be in the other person's Shoes.

To really step into someone else's Shoes, I tell children to think about what it would be like to be that person—to be in his current situation and to have been through what he has experienced in the past. To help your child develop this skill, you can practice with her through books, TV, movies, and real-life situations. For example, if you see a child crying at the park, you could ask your child why that child might be crying. Talk about what might have happened and what that other child might be feeling. In the grocery store, you might talk about how the cashier seemed to be really slow and making mistakes and then ask your child about being in the cashier's Shoes. Offer some reasons for the cashier's behavior and ask your child to do the same. Maybe it's the cashier's first day of work, he didn't get enough sleep the night before, or he is worried about a sick friend. When reading a book together or watching TV, you can ask your child what a character might be feeling by asking her to put herself in the character's Shoes and think about how she might feel in the character's situation. Model empathy for your child by telling her how you might feel if you were in that character's Shoes.

Research has shown that when mothers talked to their children about other people's feelings, beliefs, wants, and intentions, those children developed a much better social understanding than children whose mothers did not. Since children don't always have the words to label their own emotions or those of others, talking to your child about being in someone else's Shoes will not only give him the vocabulary he needs but will also help them to be more empathetic. For example, if your young child grabs a toy away from another child, instead of just saying "Don't grab" or "Give it back," you might say, "Look at that boy, and how do you think he might be feeling after you took his toy away?" If your child doesn't know how to respond you can ask, "Do you think he looks happy or sad?"

Step 2—Listen with your Ears, Eyes, and Heart

Step 2 gives children tangible ways to improve their empathic listening skills. Telling children to listen with their ears, eyes, and heart gives them the signal that it takes more than their ears for them to truly hear, feel, and understand the other person. It's helpful to remind your child to practice his *Ninja Breathing* while listening to the other person. *Ninja Breathing* will help to keep your child present and focused on what the other person is saying.

Listening with your eyes means you are asking your child to keep her eyes on the person who is speaking. To practice this at home, stand in front of your child and ask her to tell you something while you purposefully look away. Then switch roles and ask your child to stand in front of you and then listen to you while looking to the side. Usually, it's very obvious to children that not looking directly at someone makes it much more difficult to really focus, listen, and understand what the other person is saying.

Since body language plays a major role in communication,

listening with your eyes will also help your child have greater insight into what the other person is saying. You can tell your child to look for cues such as facial expressions, body posture, gestures, and eye movement. You can help him read body language when you practice the exercises for learning empathy. For example, you might be with your child at the post office and see a man in the line next to you who is frowning and incessantly tapping his foot. You and your child can play a game to create suggestions about what the man might be communicating through his body language—impatience, frustration, etc.

Listening with your heart is not quite as easy to demonstrate, but it's a key element to learning empathy. I explain to children that listening with their heart means that they are showing the other person that the most important thing at that moment is listening to that person. It's about staying open to really hearing and understanding the other person. That means making sure the other person feels safe with you and doesn't feel that you are disinterested or judging. A helpful tip for your child is to explain that if she is standing with her arms crossed and looking away or down, she is most likely not in her heart and is showing the other person that she is not interested in what that person is saying. I explain to children that remarks like "Yeah" and "Uh huh" can also signal that they are not really listening, while rolling their eyes and making snide remarks like "Ugh!" or the ever popular "Whatevvver!" are clear signs that they are judging the other person and are certainly not in their heart.

Step 3—Open Your Mind and Close Your Mouth

Step 3 is often the most challenging—not just for children but for most people. Even if we are able to keep our mouths shut, our minds are often working at warp speed to prepare our response. Even though this is a tricky one, children can learn from an early age to open their mind and close their mouth.

Opening your mind is about putting aside your own judgments, ideas, and opinions about what the other person is saying so that you can truly understand that person. I like to use the analogy of colored sunglasses to help children understand this concept. I tell them to imagine that they are wearing blue-tinted sunglasses and the person they are listening to is wearing rose-tinted sunglasses. With their blue-tinted sunglasses, they are seeing the world through a blue filter, while their friend is seeing the world through a rose filter. In order to really open their mind, they need to remove their blue-tinted sunglasses. It doesn't mean they have to wear rose-tinted glasses forever, but they can at least try to see the world through their friend's rose filter.

Very often when people are talking, no one is really listening. Everyone is just taking turns speaking. Generally most people are more interested in voicing their own views than really listening and understanding others. So the close your mouth part will take some practice, but children can definitely learn to respect others when others are talking, and this skill will be invaluable to them as they grow into adults.

OUR SHOES

The final component to My Shoes, Your Shoes, Our Shoes teaches children to work together with others in a way that respects everyone's thoughts and feelings. I don't think anyone needs a research study to know that this skill will have value for your child in all areas and stages in his life—from sibling relationships to friendships to romantic partnerships, and from classroom to family room to boardroom.

The approach of Our Shoes encourages children to look for connections to other people instead of focusing on feeling separate or different. It's a way of looking to others with a spirit of cooperation instead of competition.

To wrap up our story of the third-grade class project, the final step was to talk through Our Shoes. Once Mandy had expressed herself in My Shoes and the boys had truly heard her and empathized with her in Your Shoes, they were ready to work together to find a solution. At this point, Our Shoes was a natural next step. The group was actually excited to find a restaurant that would work for everyone, including their vegetarian friend, and when the three students together decided on a choice, they all felt really proud about how they had resolved their conflict.

Working as a team is part of human nature. No man is an island, remember? It's in our nature to want to live together, play together, and work together. It's not always easy and it's not always smooth, but giving your child the skills to Our Shoes will give her a much better shot at a connected life.

STEPS TO OUR SHOES

The steps to Our Shoes are very basic, but when applied they are very powerful.

1. Respect each other's feelings and opinions

2. Work together to find a solution or understanding

Step 1—Respect Each Other's Feelings and Opinions

The first step to Our Shoes helps children to value differences and deepen their acceptance of others. This step requires that children understand that not everyone sees the world as they do. I like to explain that even good friends can have different opinions and can disagree, but that it's very important to respect each other's feelings and opinions. I tell children that it's about understanding their needs as well as the needs of others.

In teaching this step, I like to use the analogy of the martial arts bow. Before students do any kind of partner work, they bow to each other. In my school, this bow means that they will be a good friend to themselves and a good friend to their partner. It's a sign of mutual respect. After they have worked together, they bow once again. This time the bow signifies gratitude toward the other person, thanking him for being a good friend. While I don't ask my non-martial arts students to use the bow, I do ask them to think of the meaning of the bow and how they can approach their lives from a place of respect and understanding of others.

After learning My Shoes, Your Shoes, Our Shoes, an eight-year-old boy was very excited to share his personal story with me. He told me that his family had gone to an amusement park that past weekend and that he and his younger brother were waiting in line to ride a roller coaster. He was really looking forward to the ride and was eager to get to the front of the line. He then glanced at his brother and saw that his brother looked scared and hesitant. He said his first impulse was to yell, "Chicken!" (Having grown up with three brothers, I know that type of reaction all too well.) But then he told me that before he acted on that impulse he thought about what it would be like to be in his brother's Shoes, to be so young and to be in line for a pretty scary ride. He realized that his brother was younger than him, and he wanted to understand and respect his brother's feelings. So he suggested they leave that line and walk over to a less scary roller coaster. I was really humbled by this story. I loved that he used this Tool for Life without any adult intervention, and without having a big discussion or debate with his brother. It all came from within, and he was genuinely happy to have discovered and applied Our Shoes.

Step 2 — Work Together to Find a Solution or Understanding

As my students in the third-grade group project illustrated, if you really go through the steps of My Shoes and Your Shoes, the final step of Our Shoes is often quite natural and easy. I tell children that this step is about learning to find a solution that honors everyone's needs. A great way to do this is for everyone involved to come up with ideas and suggestions. It is important that everyone gets a chance to voice ideas and then as a team decide which plan is best. Children even as young as age four are able to suggest solutions to problems with other children.

Depending on the age and situation of the child, I sometimes add to my explanation of step 2 that the solution never requires violating emotional or physical safety. The solution should always be something the child can tell a grown-up, and the child should never be asked to keep the solution a secret.

A typical occurrence in my classes is for a student to ask for a different wrestling partner because the current partner is going too hard, too fast, too soft, or too slow. I use this opportunity to explain that in life they will be interacting with all different kinds of people, and that it's important to learn to communicate and work with people who do things differently than they do. I then use their wrestling exercise as a mini-life workshop by asking them to see if they can figure out how to wrestle together in a way that's both fun and beneficial for both of them. Very regularly the students find a solution on their own to make it work.

MY SHOES, YOUR SHOES, OUR SHOES FOR CONFLICT RESOLUTION

Each component of My Shoes, Your Shoes, Our Shoes teaches children an important social skill: My Shoes—to clearly express themselves; Your Shoes—to listen and understand what it feels like to be someone else; Our Shoes—to work with others with mutual respect. These three components work independently of one another and yet they work together beautifully as a process. You will find times when it's useful to remind your child of just one of the components, and you will find times when the whole process is necessary.

For example, at the dinner table your child might be telling you about something that happened on the playground at school. The child might be overly excited and upset, perhaps blaming others, perhaps shut down. By using My Shoes, you can help her to clearly explain herself so that she can better understand what happened and how she feels about it. You might not need to go through the whole process of Your Shoes and Our Shoes.

On the other hand, you might be facilitating a disagreement between siblings and find you need a process for conflict resolution. In this case, suggest trying My Shoes, Your Shoes, Our Shoes. Explain that this Tool for Life isn't about proving who is right or wrong or about someone getting in trouble but that it's about learning to be understood, to understand others, and to work together to find a resolution. Let them know that both of them will get enough time to explain their own Shoes. If neither volunteers, I find it helpful to let them know that you understand that both would like to speak first and to assure them that they will both get a chance. Asking again usually produces a volunteer.

Then begin with one child going through My Shoes and clearly explaining how it feels to be him in this situation. Encourage him to use his *Ninja Breathing* and be like a River while talking, and remind him that this will help the other person hear him better. Ask him not to blame the other person and to try to talk only about the current situation and not the past or unrelated issues. Ask the child to let you know when he has finished expressing My Shoes.

Encourage the child who is listening to be in Your Shoes with the goal of really trying to understand the needs and feelings of the child who is talking. You can suggest that she also use her *Ninja Breathing* to quietly listen and to use her eyes, ears, and heart to focus on the other person. Remind her that in order to really listen and understand the other person, she should try not to think about what she is going to say when it's her turn to talk. When the child speaking is finished, you can ask the listening child to repeat back what she heard and to say in her own words how the other person might be feeling. Ask the speaker to acknowledge that what the listener repeated back was accurate. He can then give feedback to clear up his point of view, if necessary. By asking the listener to repeat what she heard, it ensures to the speaker that he was heard and understood, and it helps the listener to be more empathetic and compassionate. Then switch the roles of speaker and listener using the My Shoes and Your Shoes steps.

Once both children feel heard and understood, you can work on Our Shoes to find a solution or understanding that honors both children. If you notice that they both had similar feelings such as hurt or anger, you can ask if they can see what feelings they had in common, encouraging a connection between them. Then you can ask both for suggestions to resolve the issue and how to prevent it or deal with it in the future. After they have generated ideas, you can help them evaluate by asking, "What might happen if you _____?" or "How might he/she feel if you _____?" Try to refrain from judging ideas or giving your own solution unless it's absolutely necessary. It is more empowering to help the children evaluate the ideas themselves and see why they may work or not work.

Once an Our Shoes solution has been reached, ask each child to verbalize it so that the agreement is clear. If there is not a specific problem to resolve but rather just hurt feelings, ask if they both feel heard and understood. You can remind them that they can agree to disagree and that even if they can't find a specific solution, they can still respect and honor each other's feelings and opinions.

There are a few ways for you to wrap it up. Ask both children if there is anything else they would like to say before moving on. Ask each child if he or she feels better after having gone through the My Shoes, Your Shoes, Our Shoes process. Take a moment for both children to acknowledge and appreciate what they experienced in themselves or others, such as honesty, courage, patience, compromise, or respect. In the end, this process should feel like a safe and empowering way for children to resolve conflicts.

Don't worry about following this conflict resolution outline perfectly. It's more important to understand the principles behind it. Plus the more you use this process with your child, the more natural it will become for both of you.

PARENTING PILLARS

Let's take a look at how the Life Ki-do Parenting Pillars—Modeling, Unconditional Love and Acceptance, Nurturing and Empowering Encouragement, and Empowering Discipline—can help you to teach your child My Shoes, Your Shoes, Our Shoes.

By this point, you have seen over and over how your child learns so much from what you do and not just what you tell him to do. So in **Modeling** My Shoes, Your Shoes, Our Shoes, you can explicitly follow the three-step process of the tool or you can simply apply the overall philosophy. The main point is that your children see you clearly expressing yourself without screaming or blaming others, really listening to others with your heart and with the intention of understanding their perspective, and working together with your children or with others with a team approach mind-set.

In order to express herself with strength and confidence in My Shoes and to respect her own feelings and opinions in Our Shoes, a child needs to really love and accept herself. As we know, giving your child **Unconditional Love and Acceptance** will undoubtedly get her on the right track.

Applying **Nurturing and Empowering Encouragement** is important when using this Tool for Life because while you want your children to feel nurtured and understood, you also need to provide the encouragement and space to come up with their own solutions. Having children work together to problem solve rather than you, as the parent, stepping in to control the situation, boosts the confidence of the children and helps them learn to resolve their own conflicts in the future without your assistance. In addition, a solution that comes from the children rather than the grown-ups is more likely to be implemented because the children feel a sense of ownership.

But it's important that the children feel you care about the situation even though you are asking them to find a solution. Try to be sensitive enough to know how much or how little input you should give. Sometimes your best role is to ask questions: "Does it seem to you that you are being understood?" "Do you both agree that this Our Shoes solution works?"

My Shoes, Your Shoes, Our Shoes can be a useful tool in **Empowering Discipline**. It can be used when you want your child to really understand his behavior and hear how it affected someone else, whether that be a friend, a parent, or the family team as a whole. It can also be used for the child to come up with his own solution to a problem, mistake, or misbehavior instead of you issuing punishments in which the child has no input. Not only will this tool help the child self-evaluate, but it will also help the child take more ownership for correcting the situation because he is a part of coming up with a solution. At the least, this tool will provide the child with an understanding of how better to deal with the situation if it arises again.

MY SHOES, YOUR SHOES, OUR SHOES SUMMARY

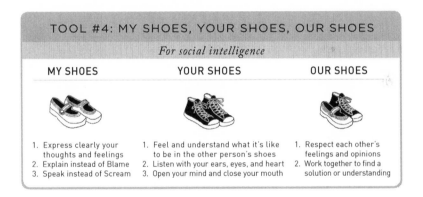

TOOL #4: MY SHOES, YOUR SHOES, OUR SHOES		
For social intelligence		
MY SHOES	**YOUR SHOES**	**OUR SHOES**
1. Express clearly your thoughts and feelings	1. Feel and understand what it's like to be in the other person's shoes	1. Respect each other's feelings and opinions
2. Explain instead of Blame	2. Listen with your ears, eyes, and heart	2. Work together to find a solution or understanding
3. Speak instead of Scream	3. Open your mind and close your mouth	

TOOLS FOR LIFE SUMMARY

To help you remember all of the Tools for Life, the following is an outline of the Tools and their individual steps.

TOOL #1: RIVER CHECK-IN—3 Bs

For focus and mindfulness

BODY	BREATH	BRAIN
BODY CHECK	BREATH CHECK	BRAIN CHECK

BODY CHECK

1. Spine—long and strong
2. Muscles—not too tight, not too loose, but in the middle like a river

BREATH CHECK

1. Ninja Breathing—To calm and de-stress
   • Slow, deep breaths in the nose and out the MOUTH
2. Fire Breathing—To energize and focus
   • Fast, short breaths in the nose and out the NOSE
3. River Breathing—To focus and feel good
   • Slow, deep breaths in the nose and out the NOSE

BRAIN CHECK

1. Focus on what you are doing using your:
   • Brain
   • Eyes
   • Ears

TOOL #2: RIVER EFFORT—ICE, PUDDLE, RIVER

For confidence and a strong sense of self

ICE	PUDDLE	RIVER

ICE

1. Trying too much
2. Feeling stuck, pressured, or stressed

PUDDLE

1. Trying too little
2. Feeling dull, lazy, or bored

RIVER

1. Putting your heart into what you are doing and giving it your all
2. Feeling happy, confident, and fulfilled

TOOL #3: A-B FORMULA

For resilience and the ability to deal with life's challenges

A = ACCEPT	B = BABY STEP
1. Be aware of where you are today 2. Be kind and patient with yourself 3. Take responsibility instead of blaming others	1. Take a step in the direction you want to go 2. Make it a step you can handle today

TOOL #4: MY SHOES, YOUR SHOES, OUR SHOES

For social intelligence

MY SHOES	YOUR SHOES	OUR SHOES
1. Express clearly your thoughts and feelings 2. Explain instead of Blame 3. Speak instead of Scream	1. Feel and understand what it's like to be in the other person's shoes 2. Listen with your ears, eyes, and heart 3. Open your mind and close your mouth	1. Respect each other's feelings and opinions 2. Work together to find a solution or understanding

CHAPTER 7

THE WHEEL OF LIFE KI-DO

It is easier to build strong children than to repair broken men.
—Frederick Douglass

Frederick Douglass, author of the above quote and an American social reformer, orator, and statesman, lived in the 1800s, yet the truth he spoke is just as poignant today. Unfortunately, however, many children in the modern world are not receiving the strong foundation they need, resulting in many broken adults searching for their inner strength and happiness. Today's booming $11 billion self-help industry is clear evidence of the overwhelming number of adults looking for ways to repair and reconstruct. With so much pressure, stress, and anxiety in today's world, children need an inner navigation system that they can rely on. Now is the time to give your child a strong foundation. The longer you wait the more your child will have to repair later on.

As one mom explained it, the reason my Life Ki-do martial arts classes are so popular and often have long waiting lists is that "the kids are definitely learning far more than kicking and punching! They are learning life lessons of great value!" Parents know their children will learn the life skills necessary to build a strong foundation. Now your child has the same opportunity. This book has given you a clear blueprint to build a happy and confident child. Teach your child the Tools for Life to give her the foundation she needs for today and into adulthood. What greater gift can you give your child?

It took me years and years to unglue myself from the American Happiness Formula (Look Good + Perform Well + Get Approval = Happiness). It stole years from my life and almost took the life of my brother. While the American Happiness Formula taught us to look for happiness from the outside in, the Life Ki-do Tools for Life system gives children the infrastructure to find happiness from the inside out.

Giving your child the means to develop his happiness from the inside out will give him deep roots—the kind of roots that are not easily swayed by the winds of peer pressure and negative influences, the kind of roots that will not snap at adversity or stress but will bounce back with resilience, the kind of roots from which a strong human being will blossom. Without this deep foundation, your child could very easily become another adult living on shaky ground without roots to stand on and wings to fly.

HOW TO BEGIN

Yes, giving your child a foundation of inner strength and happiness is critical, yet the beauty of the Tools for Life system is that it's so simple. Instead of seeing this as another big project you need to add to your busy life, see it as a way to bring a new perspective to what you are already doing. Over time, the tools should become a default operating system for your family. Remember the second grader who said, "I use these tools so much that I forget I'm using them!"

How should you begin? Take the A–B Formula approach. Accept that where you are today is a great place to start. Then choose one Baby Step based on your comfort level and family dynamics. If you feel that your child will be open and receptive, take the team approach by together choosing one tool or even just one step under one tool to begin. If you feel you might be met with some resistance from your child, I suggest that you choose one tool and practice it yourself before introducing it to your child. By modeling the tool before teaching it to your child, you not only will be a living example of the benefits, but you will be able to speak about the tool from your own firsthand experience. In addition, a resistant child will be more open to the tools if she sees you genuinely trying to improve yourself and your relationship with her rather than trying to fix or change her. This will open the door to the team approach.

Once you have decided on a tool or step to begin, use it across the board—at mealtime, homework time, playtime, and bedtime. You'll find that the tools are easily plugged in to all areas of your family life.

To create the best environment for your child to learn and implement the Tools for Life, my best advice is not only to practice them yourself but to be aware of implementing the four Parenting Pillars.

The four Parenting Pillars were actually born out of the four Tools for Life, so they work hand in hand, and with some practice they will all become integrated. It will be a new but natural way of life for you and your family. Not just a false or superficial state of happiness but a deep, peaceful, and fulfilled way of living.

WHEEL OF LIFE KI-DO

At Life Ki-do's hub is ancient wisdom for modern living. I have distilled the ancient wisdom of warriors and wise men into a simple, practical, and relevant system for today's world. While this book presents that wisdom in kid-friendly terms for you to teach your child, the principles are so universal that they are valuable to anyone of any age.

Over the years there have been a number of students who started in my classes at age four or five and continued all the way until they graduated high school and beyond. These students are perfect examples of the Wheel of Life Ki-do. While the presentation of the life-skill curriculum evolved in age-appropriate increments, the same principles were always at the heart of the training. One mom wrote after her son graduated from high school, "My son was a shy, bullied boy, and thanks to you and Life Ki-do he has become a strong, calm, centered, confident man. I fully believe in the transformative powers of your program and recommend it to everyone. You reach down into the heart and soul of the student, and through hard work and dedication they become better individuals from the inside out."

Of course, my own life is a testament to the same. The Tools for Life have truly become the rock and foundation of my life—of the inner strength and inner happiness I have uncovered. I have used the tools in all areas of my life, from the most mundane to the most profound, and they have truly made me a better father, husband, son, brother, and friend.

Without a doubt, one of the most profound moments of my life was the moment my mother took her last breath. She and I had always been close as mother and son, but over the years our relationship evolved into a true friendship. We were very much alike, and I think she was very proud that I was able to break out of the American Happiness Formula. She admired and respected my search for inner strength and happiness, and she regularly asked me to share with her what I had discovered. She was also a great seeker of inner peace and happiness, and unfortunately, like so many, her journey included a battle with cancer. As her time neared, she reached out to me for strength and support to face death. I had no experience with the end of life, and being that she was one of the closest people to me, it was understandably a devastating time.

However, the Tools for Life allowed me to help my mother face her fears, and they allowed me to be totally present, in my heart, and deeply connected to her as she took her very last breath. I relied on the A–B Formula over and over again to accept the terribly sad situation and to find Baby Steps to have the strength and resilience to be present and available to her instead of being overtaken by sadness. Of course, there were times when I was overwhelmed by stress, fear, and sadness, and my Body, Breath, and Brain felt like Ice. But I constantly returned to a River state, knowing it would allow me to best support my mother. I was able to rely on the empathy and compassion I had cultivated with Your Shoes to genuinely encourage her to let go rather than selfishly telling her to hang on and not leave us. As a family, we were able to practice Our Shoes by honoring her wishes to be at home surrounded by her loved ones. I dearly miss my mother, and it was truly an honor and a privilege to be part of that sacred moment. I feel so fortunate that my years of life-skill training allowed me to hold my mother's hand, look into her eyes, and give her all the love and support she needed and so deserved as she took her last breath.

A few years later, I was able to use the tools in one of the other most profound and momentous occasions of my life—the moment my daughter took her first breath. As many births go, nothing was going as planned and my wife needed an unscheduled C-section. Her hopes of having the baby placed in her arms immediately after the birth were wiped away, as she was on the operating table with complications. My wife had always insisted that I go with the baby no matter what, so I escorted our minutes-old daughter to the nursery. My wife would not be our little girl's first human connection. I would. It was overwhelming and scary.

But without consciously thinking about it, the tools kicked in. I connected to the Breath, opened my heart, and felt the River strength, happiness, joy, and love flood in. My daughter and I locked eyes for what seemed like an eternal moment. Turns out it was actually forty-five minutes, which I understood later was an unusually long time for a just born baby to be so awake and directly focused and engaged. It was an unbelievably precious moment filled with utter awe, joy, and love. Without the tools I would never have been able to give my daughter such a sacred and intimate welcome into the world.

If you are reading this book, you are most likely a parent as well and have experienced your own magical moment the first time you laid eyes on your child. I know that all I could ever want as a parent is for my child to be healthy and happy, and I'm sure you wish the same for yours. With all my heart, I hope this book gives you the ancient wisdom and modern blueprint to raise a happy, confident child from the inside out.

NOTES

Chapter 1

1. S. Jay Olshansky, Douglas J. Passaro, Ronald C. Hershow, Jennifer Layden, Bruce A. Carnes, Jacob Brody, Leonard Hayflick, Robert N. Butler, David B. Allison, and David S. Ludwig, "A potential decline in life expectancy in the United States in the 21st century," *New England Journal of Medicine* 352, no. 11 (2005): 1138–1145.

2. Jean M. Twenge et al., "Birth cohort increases in psychopathology among young Americans, 1938–2007: A cross-temporal meta-analysis of the MMPI," *Clinical Psychology Review* 30, no. 2 (2010): 145–154.

3. Jean M. Twenge, *Generation Me: Why Today's Young Americans Are More Confident, Assertive, Entitled—and More Miserable Than Ever Before* (New York: Free Press, 2006), 108, 117–119.

4. Jean M. Twenge et al., "It's beyond my control: A cross-temporal meta-analysis of increasing externality in locus of control, 1960–2002," *Personality and Social Psychology Review* 8, no. 3 (2004): 308–319.

5. Richard M. Ryan and Edward L. Deci, "Self-determination theory and the facilitation of intrinsic motivation, social development, and well-being," *American Psychologist* 55, no. 1 (2000): 68–78.

6. Edward Diener and Martin E. P. Seligman, "Very happy people," *Psychological Science* 13, no. 1 (2002): 81–84.

7. Claudia Wallis, "The science of happiness turns 10. What has it taught?" *Time*, July 8, 2009.

Chapter 2

1. Richard M. Ryan and Edward L. Deci, "Self-determination theory and the facilitation of intrinsic motivation, social development, and well-being," *American Psychologist* 55, no. 1 (2000): 68–78.

2. Edward L. Deci, Richard Koestner, and Richard M. Ryan, "A meta-analytic review of experiments examining the effects of extrinsic rewards on intrinsic motivation," *Psychological Bulletin* 125, no. 6 (1999): 627–668.

3. Mark R. Lepper, David Greene, and Richard E. Nisbett, "Undermining children's intrinsic interest with extrinsic reward: A test of the 'overjustification' hypothesis," *Journal of Personality and Social Psychology* 28, no. 1 (1973): 129–137.

4. Sloan Wilson, *What Shall We Wear to This Party?: The Man in the Gray Flannel Suit Twenty Years Before & After.* (New York: Arbor House, 1976).

5. Jane Nelsen, *Positive Discipline* (New York: Ballantine Books, 2006), 14.

Chapter 3

1. Kirk Warren Brown, Richard M. Ryan, and J. David Creswell, "Mindfulness: Theoretical foundations and evidence for its salutary effects," *Psychological Inquiry* 18, no. 4 (2007): 211–237.

2. "Health hint: Breathing exercises," adapted from David Rakel, *Integrative Medicine* (Philadelphia: Saunders, 2003). www.amsa. org/healingthehealer/breathing.cfm.

3. Andrew Newberg and Mark Robert Waldman, *How God Changes Your Brain: Breakthrough Findings from a Leading Neuroscientist* (New York: Ballantine Books, 2009), 179–182.

4. Ibid.

5. Susan Kaiser Greenland, *The Mindful Child: How to Help Your Kid Manage Stress and Become Happier, Kinder, and More Compassionate* (New York: Free Press, 2010), 91.

Chapter 4

1. Claudia M. Mueller and Carol S. Dweck, "Praise for intelligence can undermine children's motivation and performance," *Journal of Personality and Social Psychology* 75, no. 1 (1998): 33–52.

Chapter 5

1. Tuppett Yates, Byron Egeland, and L. Alan Sroufe, "Rethinking resilience: A developmental process perspective," in *Resilience and Vulnerability: Adaptation in the Context of Childhood Adversities*, ed. Suniya S. Luthar, 234–256 (New York: Cambridge University Press, 2003).

2. Nathaniel Branden, *The Six Pillars of Self-Esteem*. (New York: Bantam Books, 1995), 93.

3. Martin E. P. Seligman, *The Optimistic Child: A Proven Program to Safeguard Children Against Depression and Build Lifelong Resilience* (New York: Houghton Mifflin, 2007), 58.

4. Carol S. Dweck, *Mindset: The New Psychology of Success*. (New York: Ballantine Books, 2008).

5. Jim Loehr and Tony Schwartz, *The Power of Full Engagement: Managing Energy, Not Time, Is the Key to High Performance and Personal Renewal* (New York: Free Press, 2003), 178.

Chapter 6

1. Andrew Newberg and Mark Robert Waldman, *How God Changes Your Brain: Breakthrough Findings from a Leading Neuroscientist* (New York: Ballantine Books, 2009), 179–182.

2. Joshua Wolf Shenk, "What makes us happy?" *The Atlantic*, June 2009.

3. George Vaillant, "Yes, I stand by my words, 'happiness equals love—full stop,'" *Positive Psychology News Daily*,

July 16, 2009, http://positivepsychologynews.com/news/
george-vaillant/200907163163.

4. Mark D. Holder, Ben Coleman, and Judi M. Wallace, "Spiritu-
    ality, religiousness, and happiness in children aged 8–12 years,"
    Journal of Happiness Studies 11, no. 2 (2010): 131–150.

5. Edward Diener and Martin E. P. Seligman, "Very happy
    people," *Psychological Science* 13, no. 1 (2002): 81–84.

6. Martin E. P. Seligman, *Flourish: A Visionary New Understanding
    of Happiness and Well-being* (New York: Free Press, 2011).

7. Diane Ackerman, "The brain on love," *New York Times*, March
    25, 2012.

Photographers of West Lake

ABOUT THE AUTHORS

Jonathan Hewitt is founder of Life Ki-do Parenting, Martial Arts, and Life Education. Jonathan has been teaching martial arts and life skills to children age three to nineteen for over twenty years and has a renowned martial arts academy in Austin, Texas. He has a degree in psychology from Emory University and has spent the past twenty-five years in intensive study of and training in meditation, mindfulness, and the brain-body connection. His great joy comes from sharing ancient, universal life skills to inspire and empower children, teens, and parents to discover and live from their inner strength.

Lana Hewitt, Jonathan's wife, also has many years of study in meditation and mindfulness, as well as a background in design and marketing, helping to bring the work of Life Ki-do to light. She is co-author, co-creator, and co-founder of Life Ki-do.

Their greatest collaboration to date is their daughter Emilia who melts their hearts daily.

For more information about our programs,
please visit www.lifekido.com